African Universities
and Western Tradition

THE GODKIN LECTURES
AT HARVARD UNIVERSITY

1964

*The Godkin Lectures on the Essentials of
Free Government and the Duties of the Citizen
were established at Harvard University in 1903
in memory of Edwin Lawrence Godkin (1831–1902).
They are given annually under the auspices of the
Harvard Graduate School of Public Administration.*

African Universities and Western Tradition

· BY ERIC ASHBY

Master of Clare College, University of Cambridge

HARVARD UNIVERSITY PRESS

CAMBRIDGE, MASSACHUSETTS · 1964

Preface

In the entrance hall of the Queen's University of Belfast there is a memorial to Edwin Lawrence Godkin. He was a student there and founder-president of the college debating society which still flourishes. This society provided Godkin's first encounter with the general theme of these annual lectures: "the essentials of free government and the duties of the citizen"; for one of the constraints imposed on the society was that it should not discuss politics or religion, and there is reason to believe that Godkin did not succumb to this constraint.

Godkin's intellectual courage and independence of thought received their first trial when he was a student in an Irish university. Students in Africa find in their universities a similar testing ground for these virtues. Already, Western education has changed the patterns of thought all over Africa; at the same time, the forces arising from African nationalism are changing the patterns of Western education. In this book, based on the Godkin Lectures delivered at Harvard University on April 7, 8, and 9, 1964, I reflect on the interaction of higher education and African society as I have studied it in Ghana and Nigeria.

The lectures could not have been prepared without help. I am particularly grateful to my friend Dr. E. A. Shils, who read the whole of the typescript and made many perceptive comments and criticisms. It is a pleasure to record my thanks to my colleague in this work, Dr. Mary Anderson, who assembled many of the facts which I use, corrected errors in the draft, and moderated some of my prejudices. For such errors and prejudices as remain I alone am responsible. Both Dr. Anderson and I wish to thank Carnegie Corporation of New York, which is supporting a study we are making of patterns of universities in some non-European societies. Finally I wish to thank Mr. Max Hall, of Harvard University Press, for his perceptive and discriminating editorial suggestions.

ERIC ASHBY

April 1964

Contents

African Universities
and Western Tradition

I. The European Tradition Exported

THE THEME

I begin with two quotations:

> We must emphatically declare that the education which we desire to see extended in India is that which has for its object the diffusion of the improved arts, science, philosophy and literature of Europe; in short of European knowledge.

> The University of Ghana shall take its place among the foremost universities of the world . . . As a great African seat of learning, it shall give leadership to African thought, scholarship and development . . .

The first of these quotations is from the despatch to the governor general of India which led to the establishment of universities in Calcutta, Bombay, and Madras; the second is from a draft charter for the University of Ghana. The one was written in 1854, the other in 1959. They are separated by a remarkable century in the history of British higher education overseas. My purpose is to spin a web between the attitudes of mind in these two quotations.

The quotations announce the theme: cultural nationalism and universities. To reduce the theme to manageable proportions, I shall draw material mainly from the English-speaking countries of West Africa. Nationalism means different things to different people: one of the meanings which the Oxford dictionary ascribes to it is "another word for egotism," a meaning which suits my theme as well as any. In the past one of the symptoms of British cultural nationalism has been an invincible confidence in the efficacy of British education, not only for home consumption but for export; not only for Englishmen but for Indians, Africans, Malayans and—for that matter—Americans. It was Macaulay who wanted to create in India "a class of persons Indian in blood and colour, but English in tastes, in opinions, in morals and in intellect." For a time the Indian intellectuals were his strongest ally in this endeavour. English was deemed more significant than Sanskrit; Shakespeare more relevant than the Mahabharata; the teaching of Milton and Burke more appropriate than the teaching of Buddha. Inevitably Macaulay's wish came true: the "persons Indian in blood and colour" discovered, running through page after page of English literature, a golden thread of freedom and liberty. Indian nationalism was born in the rooms of university students, first in London and Cambridge, then in the universities of India. Its first language was English. Its first teachers were British. What could you expect an Indian to think, as he read Burke's words at the trial of Warren Hastings: "If we undertake to govern the inhabitants of such a country, we must govern them upon their own principles and maxims, and not upon ours. We must not think to force them into the narrow circle of our ideas; we must extend ours to take in their system of opinions and rites . . ."[1]

From the graduates of the universities the currents of nationalism flowed into the press and the people. Step by step India secured her liberty. This brought the tide of nationalism back into the Indian universities, and they began to adapt themselves to the indigenous intellectual climate; with renewed respect they turned back to their own culture.[2]

All this happened years ago. In Africa something similar is happening now. Africa has stretched the word "nationalism" to cover new meanings. At the core of an African's loyalty lie his extended family and his tribe. Outside this core his loyalty extends far beyond the frontiers of his nation; it covers the Black African people, their oral traditions and religions, their dance and music, their liberation from foreign control and their ultimate political unity. African nationalism is really an amalgam of three ingredients: loyalty to a race, loyalty to a culture (to a mystique which Dr. Nkrumah called the African personality); and a passionate distrust of foreign influences in any form: imperialism, trusteeship, the paternalism of protectorates. It, too, was born in America and Britain: in the editorial room of the *African Interpreter*, published by African students in the United States, at meetings of the West African Students' Union in London, in Paris cafés. Its sources of inspiration were Jefferson and Lincoln, J. A. Hobson and the Fabians. It grew into a popular movement in the newspapers and election platforms and gaols of West Africa. African universities, built by the British, French, and Belgians on the foundations of European culture, are now being invaded by ideas and aspirations which have their source in African nationalism. We are witnessing in Africa the beginning of a climacteric in the history of higher education. We are able to watch universities as they evolve to become viable in a strange and stormy intellectual climate. I invite you in this book to reflect on these events.

THE MODEL

Britain's first enterprise in the export of higher education began in Cambridge, Massachusetts. The Laws Liberties and Orders of Harvard College, published over three centuries ago, had their origin in the Elizabethan statutes of the University of Cambridge. The qualifications for entry were copied from Cambridge: the statutes of Harvard for 1646 begin: "When any Scholar is able . . . to speak Latin in verse and prose, and decline perfectly the paradigms of nouns and verbs in the Greek tongue, then may he be admitted into the College." But even when British universities were exported together with British emigrants, the universities were obliged to shape themselves to a new cultural climate. Nearly a century ago, when C. W. Eliot became president of Harvard, he wrote: "A university . . . must grow from seed. It cannot be transplanted from England or Germany in full leaf and bearing . . . When the American university appears, it will not be a copy of foreign institutions . . . but the slow and natural outgrowth of American social and political habits."[3]

Eliot's prophecy was correct. During the last century the American people have made major innovations in the pattern of higher education. Some of these innovations were described by the president of the University of California in the masterly Godkin Lectures he gave in 1963.[4] Now let us extend Eliot's prophecy to the universities in Ghana and Nigeria, to see where it leads us.

The pattern for higher education in these two West African countries is taken from the civic universities of England. We must begin, therefore, by studying the anatomy of those civic universities. They were born as colleges under local patronage, to provide a higher education for those who could not get it from Oxford or Cambridge— because Oxford and Cambridge, though by no means full in the mid-nineteenth century, excluded all but those who would subscribe to the tenets of the Anglican church and those (apart from a handful of scholars who could afford to pay. Moreover neither of these universities had much to offer students who wanted a utilitarian higher education. There followed, in nineteenth-century England, a fascinating interaction between the new colleges and the old universities. Manchester—through its example—stimulated Oxford to raise its academic standards and to regard research as a proper activity for dons. Oxford—through its graduates —transmitted to Manchester traditions of academic freedom and autonomous government. The two kinds of universities, one with its roots in the middle ages and the other with its roots in the industrial revolution, grew alike in certain essential features, though the differences between them are still profound. Today the essential similarities between Oxford, Cambridge, and the civic universities of England are: (i) they are all self-governing corporations, jealously guarding their autonomy; (ii) they all aspire to grant degrees of similar standard on curricula of similar content; (iii) they all make similar assumptions about the function of higher education in British society. These three similarities consti-

tute the template from which—up to the publication of the
Robbins Report in October 1963—new universities on the
British pattern, both at home and overseas, were made.

Constitution. Sovereignty in an English civic university resides in a Council of thirty to forty members. A majority
of the members are laymen, some of them representing interests such as local government or the alumni of the university,
some of them chosen for their standing in industry or in
public life. About one fifth of the members come from the
academic staff, elected to the Council by their colleagues.
The Council controls the finance and property of the university and makes formal decisions over appointments and
indeed over most of the university's business affairs. Partly
by legislation, partly by convention (for this is never fully
set out in the constitution) the effective sovereignty over
academic affairs is delegated to a Senate. The Senate consists
of the professors together with a few—perhaps one sixth of
the total—nonprofessorial members of staff. The convention
of control for academic affairs works by regulating the
direction of flow of business. It would be little short of
scandalous for the Council to issue a directive to the Senate
or to elect a professor without advice from members of the
Senate, or to interfere with policy over admissions, examinations, and curricula, notwithstanding the fact that there is a
passage in the constitution of several English universities
which empowers the Council to "give directions" to the
Senate concerning any act of the Senate which may be
reviewed, amended, referred back, controlled, or disallowed
by the Council.

Below the Senate, and usually without many delegated powers, are faculty boards and other committees only too familiar to academics. By and large it would be true to say that the established convention in the established English civic universities is that business originates at the level of departments or faculties, flows upwards to the Senate, where policy is determined by an oligarchy of professors, and comes to the Council, the body where sovereignty formally resides, as recommendations to be adopted; or, if not adopted, to be referred back for reconsideration. In all essentials, therefore, the English civic university is professor-run, but its policies are moderated by the presence of a predominantly lay Council which represents the public interest.* Also to preserve the public interest, most English civic universities have a massive Court, which may contain as many as six hundred members, who represent every institution likely to have involvements in the university: alumni, staff, schools, local authorities, religious denominations, learned societies and professional bodies. Apart from electing the chancellor (who is in British universities an ornament, not an executive) the Court has few responsibilities. It meets once a year to receive reports on the university's progress and a cup of tea.

These autonomous corporations, depending for their stability on convention rather than on legislation, receive some £100 millions each year in grants from the State. But it is not their internal constitutional structure which protects

---

* The constitutions of recently created universities in England (e.g., Sussex, East Anglia) follow this same pattern with minor variations. One of the welcome variations is to give the nonprofessorial staff more representation (up to one third) on the Senate. So it cannot be said of these new universities that they are "professor-run."

them from interference from the State; they are effectively insulated from the State because the public finance for universities is administered by an independent body (the University Grants Committee) consisting predominantly of academics. On the University Grants Committee the controllers are at one with the controlled—a characteristically British solution to an administrative problem.

Standards and Curricula. Each year in June and July professors in England take to the road. It is examination-time; every university appoints in every subject external examiners who play some part in setting the examination papers, help in marking the candidates' scripts, and come in person to assess laboratory work, to conduct oral tests, and to take part in examiners' meetings. By carrying the criteria of achievement from one university to another these external examiners ensure a common standard for degrees. For there is in Britain an approximate parity between degrees, and even between their gradations into "firsts," "upper seconds," "lower seconds," and "thirds." This adherence to an academic gold standard is jealously guarded. Hull, Southampton, Exeter: these universities do not want their degrees to be more easily gained, or to have a lower currency on the market, than degrees in Cambridge or London. Indeed this preoccupation with classifying the quality of degrees recently provoked a wry criticism in the British press: that universities were more interested in grading students than in educating them.

The pattern of curricula in British universities has consistently changed over the last two generations. There was a time when most British university students aimed at a "pass" or "general" degree, covering a range of related subjects, and only a minority specialised by taking "honours" in one subject. This is no longer true. In 1963 eighty-one per cent of the students in the universities of England and Wales were taking courses for honours degrees—about two thirds of these in one subject only.[5] The "normal" university course has become intensely specialised: the student enters to read chemistry, or history, or French, with a very small ration of time given to ancillary subjects. This obsession with specialisation is already under heavy criticism.* The University Grants Committee and the Report of the Committee on Higher Education (Robbins Report) have both had much to say about it; and there are welcome signs, in a few universities, of a broadening of the curriculum without sacrifice of the rigorous standards or the discipline in depth which are the virtues of specialisation. But—and this is the relevance of the matter for the present theme—at the time when Britain was exporting universities to tropical Africa, the fashion of specialisation was at its height.

Social Function. In the nineteenth century, at the time universities were being founded in India and Australia, higher education in Britain was not regarded as a responsibility of the State and (except in trivial ways) was not financed by the State. Nowadays higher education in Britain is a deliberate social activity of the State, financed as to ninety per cent of its expenditure from public funds.[6] Such an activity must be based on assumptions about the social philosophy of education, even though—in typically British

* The criticism does not apply to the Scottish universities, which have a long tradition of broad-based general education.

fashion—we remain silent about them. Up to the time of publication of the British government's White Paper on the Robbins Report[7] the assumption was not (as it is in the United States) that higher education should be available to all qualified candidates who want it; the assumption was that out of the pool of qualified candidates a proportion should be selected (primarily on examination-performance) and subsidised by the State for university education of very high quality under very favourable conditions. The statistical chance that a Boston boy or girl born in 1945 is now receiving full-time higher education is about 1 in 3; the equivalent chance for a London boy or girl born in 1945 is about 1 in 12. This difference is not, of course, due to differences in academic ability between Britons and Americans, nor even to differences in the ultimate level of achievement reached by the best students: it is due to a difference between our two nations in the assumptions we make about the place of higher education in our two societies. In America the degree course is an obstacle race, open to all competitors who care to enter it, in which many competitors are eliminated before the end of the race. In Britain we select a comparatively small group from among those qualified for higher education, and we sponsor this group alone.

The favourable conditions under which we in Britain educate the élite we choose to admit to universities are the result of another assumption we make over social philosophy. The British continue to regard a university education as much more than professional training. The golden mists of Jowett's Balliol still suffuse our most modern universities: the belief that, by informal contact between teacher and student, tutor and pupil, and by the device of making students reside together in small intimate units (still, in Oxford and Cambridge, locked up each night), there will result an imponderable (and unexaminable) moral education, essential for producing men of character suitable to be leaders of the people and custodians of the cultural heritage. This is one of the many legacies which Oxford and Cambridge have conferred upon the modern British universities. Consequently all British universities now lay great emphasis on residence, and the grants from local authorities which support 87 per cent of full-time university students expressly allow students to migrate away from their home towns to universities elsewhere.

Acceptance by the British government of the basic recommendation of the Robbins Committee (that "courses of higher education should be available for all those who are qualified by ability and attainment to pursue them and who wish to do so") will change the assumptions the British make about the social function of universities, though the emphasis on residence—withdrawal from the world for three years of study and community living—still remains. For our present theme it is again important to remember that universities were exported from Britain to tropical Africa on the old assumptions about social function, not on the new.

In the streets of West African cities one can distinguish at a glance the varieties of imported automobiles: Chevrolets and Austins and Volkswagens. Universities in West Africa similarly betray their origin. Those founded by the British displayed at the time of independence the three attributes I have just described. In constitution they were autonomous, deliberately detached from the State. In standards and curriculum they emphasised the thin stream of excellence and the narrow specialism. In social function they regarded themselves as restricted to an élite.

BRITISH EXPORT POLICY 1923–1945

For a century Africans have been asking for higher education in Africa. One of the first of whom we have record was James Africanus Beale Horton, a Creole from Sierra Leone, who went to Britain in 1853 to be trained in medicine under the auspices of the War Office. He took an M.D. degree and entered the army as a staff assistant surgeon. Horton began by proposing that there should be an institution to prepare African medical students before they went overseas to hospitals in Britain, but by 1868 his ideas had grown into a "University for Western Africa" with subjects ranging from classics and Hebrew to science, law, and music.[8] He even left in his will his house in Freetown to become the nucleus of a university. But nothing came of his intentions.

Horton wanted to introduce into Africa undiluted Western education; there was no place in his scheme of higher education for the incorporation of African languages, history, or culture. In 1872 another early advocate for a West African university appeared in Freetown, a picturesque character named Edward Blyden, who conducted a public correspondence with the administrator of the colony (Pope-Hennessy) couched in charmingly high-flown phrases with a liberal sprinkling of Latin quotations. Blyden gave a new dimension to the idea of an African university: he wanted the university to release the educational system from the grip of the "despotic Europeanising influences which had warped and crushed the negro mind"; he wanted it to restore cultural self-respect among Africans. Blyden's formula for achieving this, as it evolved over the years, is interesting in the light of subsequent history. He wanted to cut out of higher education the study of modern Western civilisation and to go back to its uncontaminated sources: the Greek and Latin languages and literatures. From the classics the African could draw "nourishment" without "race poison." To this he wanted to add African languages, songs and oral tradition, and a form of Christianity adapted to the African people.[9]

A third African advocate for higher education in Africa was J. E. Casely Hayford, one of the pioneers of African nationalism in the country which is now Ghana. It was largely in order to promote these wider ends that Hayford demanded an indigenous university. His proposals, published in 1911 in a quaint book called *Ethiopia Unbound*,[10] emphasise that an African university must be no "mere foreign imitation." Teaching must be in the vernacular. Scholars must be employed to translate books into Fanti. The university must be a centre of "national conservancy and evolution," yet linked to other universities overseas; not to one alone (for this would overemphasise the influence of one country on the Gold Coast) but "in working correspondence with some of the best teaching institutions in Japan, England, Germany and America."

Hayford's long campaign (it started in 1911) reached its climax in 1920 at the First Conference of Africans of British West Africa, which met in Accra; for the conference, in a memorial addressed to King George V, submitted that the time had come "to found a British West African University on such lines as would preserve in the students a sense of African Nationality."[11]

Blyden's and Hayford's proposals were brought to the notice of the British government, and Horton appealed to the government through the pages of his own book. None of their proposals were adopted. However, Blyden did have a modest vicarious success, for the Church Missionary Society, alarmed at the prospect that Blyden might succeed in persuading the British to set up a secular university, consented in 1874 (after much dragging of feet) to arrange for their theological seminary at Fourah Bay College in Sierra Leone to accept students to study secular subjects; and by 1876 it had been arranged that these students should sit for degrees in arts to be given by the University of Durham. Fourah Bay College received no public funds for this purpose. For two generations it limped on its way, short of money and even short of students, making no concession whatever in its curriculum to the African environment. Nevertheless, during this time it made a vital contribution to the intellectual life of West Africa, for it turned out African graduates who became leaders from the Gambia down to the Cameroons. But no universities appeared in West Africa. Up to the end of the second world war there were only two publicly financed institutions engaged in higher education. One was the remarkable Achimota College near Accra, which covered education from kindergarten to first-year university courses; for a short time, in engineering, its students were even eligible to take the examinations for external degrees of London University. The other was the Higher College at Yaba, near Lagos, which granted diplomas of local currency only, in medicine, engineering, and general studies.

The resistance of the British government to the pressures for universities in Africa can be traced to three causes. First, the pressures were not consistently supported by the Africans themselves. Horton, Blyden, and Hayford were ahead of their time. The great majority of their countrymen were at first indifferent to education; indeed the chiefs and hereditary rulers, protected by the British device of indirect rule, saw in education (and even in incipient African nationalism) a threat to their power. Second, it was British policy to leave education in Africa to the private enterprise of missionaries or to the budgets of colonial governments (the metropolitan government made no grant for education in Nigeria, for instance, until 1940). The colonial governments were too impoverished, and the missionaries too preoccupied with their task of combining schooling with proselytization, to devote funds or time to higher education. Finally there was a sincere conviction on the part of British officials in Whitehall and in Africa that it would be useless to build a university except on the foundation of a sound system of secondary schools—a misguided opinion, for many of the men who held it came from Oxford or Cambridge, universities which flourished centuries before there was a sound system of secondary schools in England.

Until after the first world war, therefore, the Colonial Office in London had taken only a fitful interest in the development of education in Africa. Apart from an occasional intervention, it confined itself to a routine and unimaginative control over the appropriation of local revenues to educational purposes. In the 1920's this complacent isolationism was brought to an end. Africa—the sleeping giant in the sun—was stirring. A pioneer of African liberty, the American Negro, Burghart Du Bois, managed (against inevitable opposition) to hold the first Pan-African Congress at Paris in February 1919 at the time of the Peace Conference. The Congress called on the allied powers to "establish a code of law for the protection of the natives of Africa," and to secure for Africans education, participation in government, and ownership of their land.[12] In 1920–21 the Phelps-Stokes Fund from the United States sent a commission to examine education in Africa. For thousands of readers its report was a first introduction to the education-hunger of the African people and it had a profound effect on both sides of the Atlantic.[13]

The missionaries, closer to African life than any other white men, pressed on the British government the urgent need to have an official policy for education in Africa. The government produced the conventional response: an advisory committee. It met for the first time in 1924. Its successors still meet. Its minutes and memoranda record the evolution of a British policy for education in countries which were then colonies and which now are independent states.

The advisory committee's first pronouncement was a brief and definitive statement of British policy, published as a White Paper in 1925.[14] "Education," the statement ran, "should be adapted to the mentality, aptitudes, occupations and traditions of the various peoples, conserving as far as possible all sound and healthy elements in the fabric of their social life." Do not regard this as a rosy platitude from a group of utopian academics: it was the outcome of years of practical experience; for the committee included Frederick Lugard, who had already founded a university in Hong Kong and devised the system of indirect rule in Northern Nigeria; James Currie, who had been a director of education in the Sudan; Michael Sadler, leader of the monumental Calcutta University Commission; Hanns Vischer, who had designed a school system in Northern Nigeria; and J. H. Oldham, who brought to the committee a lifetime's experience from the mission field. This emphasis on adaptation is a far cry from Macaulay, but—notwithstanding isolated experiments such as those at Achimota—it has been remarked both by British and by American experts on African sociology that a generation after this principle was announced, there is no record that it had been generally adopted.[15] The reasons for this will appear as our story proceeds.

Our concern is with higher education. For the first ten years of its existence the advisory committee did not give serious attention to universities in the colonies. Then in 1933, one of the most imaginative and experienced of its members, James Currie, produced a brief report which is an eloquent and urgent plea for the founding of universities in tropical Africa. It called for an immediate and publicly announced programme of university development; otherwise, the report said, enlightened African opinion would be alienated and British prestige in Africa would be damaged. The report was received with enthusiasm by the committee and described as full of vision. It was endorsed by the Colonial Office and circulated to all governors in East and West Africa for their views. Here the impetus was lost; it was three years before the Colonial Office received replies from all the governors. The delay was a symptom of the indifference of white administrators on the spot. The East African directors of education could not agree that the demand for higher education was "vehement," nor were they in favour of stimulating it. Colonial authorities in Nigeria were reluctant to force the pace of higher education; they thought the matter should be kept under review but the time had not yet come to take active steps. The governor of the Gold Coast was satisfied that existing facilities were adequate and feared that a sudden increase in facilities for higher education would lead to an overproduction of graduates. As the rivers of Central Australia peter out in the blazing rocks and sands of the desert, so Currie's clear and vigorous proposals ran to waste among the colonial officials in Lagos and Accra. Only from Uganda was there an encouraging response, and a commission (under Earl de la Warr) was sent out to study the possibilities of converting the school at Makerere into a place of higher education.[16] Elsewhere negotiations dragged on. By 1939 the West African Governors' Conference in Lagos had got as far as agreeing, as a long-term project, that there should be a West African university, ultimately conferring its own degrees, but not (of course) at once; for some years it should be content to take degrees in affiliation with a British university.

Then came the war. Plans for universities in Africa were put aside, but the advisory committee continued its meetings, through bombing and the threat of invasion; and long before the tide of war turned—as early as 1940—a fresh and vigorous policy for higher education overseas was being prepared. Credit for this lies chiefly with one member of the committee, H. J. Channon, a professor of biochemistry, who became dedicated to the idea of a great network of colonial universities to equip the countries of the Commonwealth for independence. He prepared a memorandum which stated eloquently the case for universities in the colonies. At his instigation two commissions were appointed in July 1943, one (under Cyril Asquith) to enquire at large into higher education in the colonies; the other (under Walter Elliot) to make recommendations on higher education in West Africa.[17] There was an overlap of membership in the two commissions; their labours were a combined operation. They both reported in 1945; at long last Britain had declared a policy for higher education in the colonies.

The Asquith Report was Britain's blueprint for the export of universities to her people overseas. In the eyes of those who have used the blueprint over the last twenty years it has become more than a mere statement of government policy: it has been elevated to the dignity of a doctrine. Policy, which should be a convenient working hypothesis, became hardened into dogma, resistant to criticism and change. People talked of the "Asquith doctrine" and referred to university colleges in Africa as "Asquith colleges." The doctrine was a vivid expression of British cultural parochialism: its basic assumption was that a university system appropriate for Europeans brought up in London and Manchester and Hull was also appropriate for Africans brought up in Lagos and Kumasi and Kampala. There is no sign that the commission considered whether the university systems to be found in Minneapolis or Manila or Tokyo might be more appropriate. In fairness to the doctrine, let it be said that it left room for some adaptation; indeed it encouraged changes in syllabus to suit African conditions and it stressed the importance of research into African languages and cultures. But the fundamental pattern of British civic universities—in constitution, in standards and curricula, in social purpose—was adopted without demur. Colonial universities were to begin as most of the provincial universities in England began: as "university colleges" which would be transmuted into universities when they acquired charters to grant their own degrees. From the outset they were to be self-governing societies, demanding from their students the same entry-standard as is demanded by London or Cambridge; following curricula which might vary in detail but must not vary in principle from the curricula of the University of London; tested by examinations approved by London and leading to London degrees awarded on the recommendation of London external examiners. And as for their social function, the colonial universities were to be completely residential, and their prime purpose was to produce "men and women with the standards of public service and capacity for leadership which self-rule requires." In short, they were, as in England, to nurture an élite.

II. Balance Sheet for Universities in West Africa

TWO TRANSPLANTATIONS

No sooner was the Asquith Report published than it was put into practice. The years 1945 to 1948 are years which will forever stand on the credit side of the balance sheet of British colonial policy. The Inter-University Council for Higher Education in the Colonies (set up in 1945 as a successor to the old advisory committee) worked with commendable speed. The government provided money. The British universities provided men and advice. The University of London cooperated splendidly by establishing a scheme of "special relationship" to give the newly formed colonial university colleges the maximum opportunities for initiative and adaptation within the framework of London degrees; the university entered into this "special relationship" with colleges in Nigeria, the Gold Coast, the Sudan, the West Indies, and Uganda. In 1948, 104 students enrolled at University College, Ibadan, and 90 students (taken over from Achimota College) at the University College of the Gold Coast. Vigorous and imaginative Englishmen were appointed as principals of these two colleges, a surprisingly good nucleus of academic staff was recruited, and an ambitious (some would say ostentatious) building programme was launched.

The pioneers in these new university colleges faced a formidable task. On each site they had to do much more than establish a university: they had to build a town, for both sites were in uncleared bush some way from the city. Roads, homes for staff, halls for students, drainage, water supply, electricity, transport, schools, even a cemetery, became the responsibility of academic administrators. The first professors had to set up standards of teaching which would qualify the students to enter for London degrees in subjects already in the London syllabus. Clearly the pioneers had no choice but to adopt the pattern of an English university. Equally clearly this was the pattern which Africans themselves wanted. The African intellectual, educated in London or Cambridge or Manchester, would have been indignant at any softening of standards, any substitution of easier options, any cheapened version of higher education. So initially there was no problem of adaptation. The African wanted a replica of the British university at its best; the expatriate staff had no other model to offer.

For ten years buildings went up, numbers increased, the machinery of administration was assembled, and the two university colleges became an accepted feature of West African society. Each created its own characteristic pattern, but both bore the unmistakable image of their British origin. Some of this was superficial, a social mimicry of the fripperies of British academic life: gowns, high tables, grace read by a scholar, assembly in combination rooms after

dinner with port assiduously passed in the proper direction.*
But the imported pattern was not just a veneer; it permeated
the whole institution: the constitution, the standards and
curriculum, the social function.

Constitution. As recommended by the Asquith Commission,
the ordinance for the Nigerian University College in Ibadan
provided for the conventional two-tier constitution of an
English civic university: a Council with some academic
representation, but composed predominantly of laymen, and
an Academic Board (equivalent to the Senate in England)
composed of all the professors and a few teachers below
professorial rank, to which the various faculty boards reported. But in practice this constitution has not worked as
an English constitution works. For one thing, the Council
could not achieve its prime purpose of reflecting Nigerian
opinion and trends of thought over higher education, for
there was in Nigeria a very small reservoir of public men
with academic experience from whom the membership of
the Council could be drawn. Although by 1959 thirteen of
its twenty-one members were Africans, the Council was
inevitably coloured in its views by the British members, who
were far more familiar than the Africans with academic
affairs. Admirable though its membership was, it could not
be regarded as a satisfactory bridge between the college
and the African public. Furthermore, the Council's views
were deeply influenced by the quinquennial visitations from

* Only recently has there been a reaction against some of these fripperies.
Students at the new university in Kumasi, Ghana, do not wear gowns, but
national dress.

Britain (these took place in 1952, 1957, and 1961) which enquired into the college's progress and advised on its development over the coming quinquennium. The membership of all three of these visitations was British (on the 1961 visitation there was a professor from McGill, but he was a Scotsman).

If Africans had too little influence at the Council table, they had still less at the table of the Academic Board. Even as late as 1961, a year after Nigeria's independence and thirteen years after the opening of the college, the Board in Ibadan (by then called Senate) had only six Africans out of its thirty members. In the English civic university this is the body to which all academic policy is delegated. It is not surprising that some leading Nigerians were apprehensive about delegating such responsibility—involving the very pattern of higher education for their future leaders—to a body on which expatriates outnumbered Africans by four to one. The zeal of expatriate professors, anxious to establish in Africa the conventions of academic freedom, was interpreted by some critics as neocolonialism; their insistence on high standards as intolerance; their engagement with British patterns of education as pedantry. And so the peculiar equilibrium between professorial senates and lay councils, which depends on mutual confidence and a silent concordat about the distribution of power, was not reproduced in Nigeria. Council and Senate came to rest at a different point of equilibrium, one in which the professors sometimes found themselves defending the British concept of a university against queries and criticisms from the African public who (without knowing precisely what they wanted) felt that the English civic university needed adaptation before it could take root in Nigerian soil. It seemed that neither the public nor the academics had sufficient confidence in the lay governing body, whose main function was to interpret the one to the other.

The University College of the Gold Coast (later to become the University College of Ghana) started off with an ordinance somewhat similar to the one which regulated University College, Ibadan, providing for a predominantly lay Council to control financial affairs, and an Academic Board to which academic policy was to be delegated. But the first principal, David Balme, superposed on this ordinance a machinery of government which was a Lilliputian version of the machinery to be found in the University of Cambridge. It was a bold and fascinating experiment, and it is very relevant to my theme, for it was a singular manifestation of faith in what a biologist would call a "vestigial character" of the European intellectual tradition.

The universities of Oxford and Cambridge, having rid themselves centuries ago of control by Church or King, are now run as self-governing communities of scholars. To initiate you into the mysteries of government of either of these universities would require a whole set of Godkin Lectures. It is sufficient for my purpose to enunciate certain basic principles as they are to be found in Cambridge. The first principle is that no-one who is not on the roll of graduates has any voice whatever in the university's affairs. The second is that sovereignty resides in all the Masters of Arts resident in Cambridge who take part in the work of the university or its colleges. And I do not mean just formal sovereignty; I mean that no measure, however trivial, can be enacted unless approved by a majority of Masters of

Arts voting—usually in person and not by ballot—in the Senate House on King's Parade on a Saturday afternoon. This mammoth assembly (if all its members turned up it would number about 1,350) is called the Regent House. It votes on important matters, such as salary scales and the founding of a medical school; it votes with equal earnestness on unimportant matters, such as whether there should be a urinal outside the Botanic Garden and the procedure to be followed at matriculation ceremonies. Each piece of business brought before the Regent House is subject to public discussion beforehand, and the discussions, which are often used as opportunities for displays of the corrosive and futile wit dear to academics, are printed and distributed.

The business of the Regent House is prepared by numerous overworked committees. Academic affairs, which elsewhere would be in the hands of a professorial senate, are in Cambridge in the hands of a body called the General Board, which (like other central committees in the university) is elected by the rank-and-file of university teachers. There is no question of an academic hierarchy. Professors and heads of departments take their chance of election along with any other M.A.'s on the roll of the Regent House. This is the third principle: that the bodies which prepare policy for the Regent House shall not be composed of the most senior and responsible officers of the university, but of democratically elected representatives of the faculties.

It was these three principles which were incorporated into the government of the University College of the Gold Coast. The College Council—the lay governing body established by law—could not be dissolved without changing the ordinance; but it could be eroded. The process of erosion began in 1951 when the lay Council agreed to meet normally only twice a year: once to receive estimates and once to receive a report. By 1954 the government of the college, still *de jure* conducted according to the ordinance, was *de facto* being conducted according to a set of bye-laws which followed with touching fidelity the archaic and exasperating procedures of the University of Cambridge. The Gold Coast government never approved these bye-laws; nor was the original ordinance (giving sovereignty to a lay Council) amended to conform to them. This working arrangement continued until 1961, when the whole constitution was swept away and replaced by a constitution dictated by the government; but that belongs to a later chapter.

Along with this singular experiment were introduced many other anachronisms and historical survivals of English academic life. The four halls of residence were made self-governing, each with its own bye-laws (no two alike) and its officers: Master, Senior Tutor, Chaplain, Steward to High Table. As in Cambridge, the halls and not the university accountant collected the students' fees. The terms (in a country with a considerable animist and Moslem population) were labelled Michaelmas, Lent, and Trinity. Grace at table was read in Latin. The purchasing officer was called a manciple.

Within the college the experiment was surprisingly successful; perhaps not altogether surprisingly, for was it not a form of government which had been viable in medieval England, when Cambridge was an isolated stronghold of learning in an underdeveloped and largely illiterate society? The trouble was that the homology between twentieth-century West Africa and medieval England broke down at several critical points. However, the experiment had merits. It involved every member of the staff (once he had reached a modest level of seniority) in the affairs of the college. It gave responsibility (at any rate responsibility to talk and criticise and vote) to African lecturers who, under the constitutions of other university colleges in tropical Africa, would have had virtually no say in policy-making. It evoked loyalty to the idea of university autonomy and responsibility for maintaining it.

But the experiment overlooked some of the differences between the intellectual and political environments of Accra and Cambridge. The chief oversight was a neglect of public relations. The public relations of the University of Cambridge are deplorable. It needs all the immense distinction of its scholars and the irresistible beauty of its buildings to overcome the image created by its complacent public pronouncements, the smug effusions of its dons in the correspondence columns of *The Times*, and the myths sedulously cultivated by Cambridge novelists and playwrights. A university in Ghana cannot afford the luxury of this cavalier attitude towards its public. It is not sufficient for it to dedicate itself in a detached way to the advancement and dissemination of knowledge; it must also persuade the public that this detached dedication is a national necessity. It must educate the public into what a university stands for. Now the channel for this essential activity of the new institution was the College Council, which brought together three senior members of the academic staff, two members from British universities, and seven distinguished Africans: judges, members of the Legislative Assembly, native rulers. This was the body which ought to have interpreted the university

to the people and the people to the university, protecting
the university against the hot winds of politics and providing
for the public a persuasive voice in one of its most precious
national institutions.

These functions—essential for a pioneer university—were
inadequately performed. The college, established now in
palatial premises on Legon Hill outside the city, drew its
skirts around its affairs and became (as an architect boasted
of its quadrangles) "inward-looking." The Council, having
been denuded of its responsibilities, could not be expected
to dedicate itself to the public relations of the college. For
four years no report from the Council was published. By
1953 the Chairman of the Council felt constrained to say at
a Council meeting that the college was suffering through
lack of authoritative public information and that something
should be done to dispel the many misconceptions which
appeared to exist. The one activity which compensated for
these deficiencies was the work of the Department of Extra-
Mural Studies. This department did succeed in bringing the
university alive to hundreds of African citizens, and its
services were frequently acknowledged with gratitude in
the Ghana press.

In 1959, David Balme's successor tried to abandon this
experimental and informal constitution and to substitute one
based on the conventional pattern of an English civic university, with authority divided between a predominantly
lay Council and a predominantly professorial Senate. His
proposals were thrown to the academic staff for discussion
and there followed two long and stormy sessions of debate.
The current of opinion in the debate was clear enough:
there was among the academics a powerful preference for

Balme's experiment and a determination not to retreat to the more conventional constitution. In the eyes of the teaching staff—both African and European—the experiment had justified itself; but we have to recollect that the staff was still essentially European: in 1959 only sixteen per cent of the academic staff was Ghanaian, and there was not a single African professor.

So when the time came for the colleges in Ibadan and Accra to break their link with London and to become independent universities, the drafts presented to their two governments were very different. Both drafts were basically English in concept and authorship: one took as its model the modern English civic university; the other was a compromise based on Balme's facsimile of the statutes and ordinances of Cambridge. Neither displayed any sign of adaptation to the African environment. As soon as these documents reached the government offices in Lagos and Accra, they were confronted with the pressures of African nationalism. The result of this confrontation is one of the themes of my third chapter.

Standards and Curricula. In standards and curricula the university colleges at Ibadan and Accra have had similar, though not identical, policies. At each college the degree was awarded by the University of London; so the graduates came out with a prescribed and guaranteed certificate of achievement. It followed from this that each college required the same high qualifications for entry to degree courses— qualifications similar to those which British candidates have to fulfil to enter Oxford, Cambridge, or London (see foot-

note, page 66). In fact the entry-requirements for the university colleges in Ibadan and Accra were more exacting
than those for the universities in Scotland and Ireland, and
much more exacting than the entry-requirements for universities in America, Canada, and Australia.* The flow of
candidates with these attainments was at times insufficient
to fill the vacant places, and this vacuum of empty beds
constituted an additional danger to the public relations of
the colleges; but even then entry standards to degree courses
were not lowered: the colleges granted concessional entry
to students to pursue preliminary courses which (if they
passed) qualified them to enter degree courses.

It can be truly said that these constraints were part of the
price willingly paid by Africans for the privilege of taking
a degree from the University of London. But the colleges
were unwilling to make full use of the flexibility allowed
them within the structure of a London degree. For example,
London gives the student a choice between a general (or
pass) degree for which he studies several subjects, or a
special (or honours) degree in which he specialises on one
(or sometimes two) subjects. I have already explained how
the pass or general degree has gone out of fashion in
England (though not altogether in Scotland) and how in
England four fifths of the students now read for honours
degrees, most of which require extreme specialisation; and
I have explained how this academic mixture is thought to

* This has some unfortunate consequences. Many young Africans who
find themselves unqualified to enter Makerere or Ibadan are offered places
in American universities and even scholarships to cover their travel and
education. And this has happened while there have been vacant places in
African university colleges.

be too rich even for Britain, and there is strong official criticism of it. Now there was no obligation upon the African universities to follow this trend. The national need in Nigeria and Ghana was for a sprinkling of highly specialised experts and scholars, and a broad stream of less differentiated graduates with general degrees to man the civil service and to teach in schools. But the desire to emulate even the fashions of British academic life was irresistible. Many of the expatriate staff, with the ready acquiescence of the Africans, encouraged specialisation. Over the years 1957–1960, for instance, in the Faculty of Arts, the University College of Ghana produced 95 graduates in single honours subjects and only 45 graduates with general degrees in Arts. In Ibadan in 1961 nearly half the Arts degrees (61 out of 125) were awarded for intensive study in one subject (including 10 in classics and 12 in English). Out of 450 Arts graduates from Ibadan in the decade up to 1961, 215 were honours specialists. In fairness to the African university colleges it must be added that the curriculum for the general degree in Arts in the University of London is lamentably unsatisfactory as an instrument of education, and is as unpopular in London as it is in Africa. So the African colleges could plead that they were forced, on educational grounds, to push their students into honours courses. But it is pretty clear from records and comments from the African colleges over ten years that they were not driven toward specialisation simply in order to avoid the admittedly unsatisfactory general degree. If confirmation of this were needed, it could be found in the pattern of courses in Arts which Ibadan University has adopted since its independence from London (see p. 68): one which entirely excludes the possibility of a broad-based education in humanities, such as the universities of Scotland have offered, and with such success, for generations.* A further factor which favours honours degrees is that African employers (again aping practice in England) offer preferential treatment and financial inducements to graduates with honours degrees, even for posts where specialisation has no relevance whatever.

In content the curriculum naturally followed the English pattern, though the University of London has been generous in encouraging, within the framework of its degree structure, substantial modifications in syllabus. African plants and animals took the place of European ones in biology courses. Papers in African history and geography were introduced. The University of London consented even to examine students in subjects which the African colleges wanted to develop; the study of government, for example, was incorporated into the degree structure at Ibadan. These were superficial—though useful—adaptations. But in some professional studies even such adaptations as these could not be made; the legacy of Britain's colonial policy was too strong. In medicine, for instance, Nigerians were still smarting under the humiliation of the Yaba diploma, which permitted a man to practice only in Nigeria, and which, although it was a six-year course of high standard, condemned the practitioner to the inferior grade of medical assistant. At the same time a Nigerian who had been lucky enough to bring back a quali-

---

* The University of Ghana has, however, recently restored a more reasonable balance between the numbers of students reading for general and honours degrees.

fication from Britain was called a medical officer, and commanded a much higher salary for similar work.* So Nigerians insisted on medical and other professional qualifications which would allow them to practice in London, not just in their own country—even though these qualifications were less appropriate to African needs. In medicine, for instance, the need—and it is a desperate need—is for men who can specialise in preventive medicine and child health. Yet students in the medical school at Ibadan (though not in the medical school at Kampala in Uganda which taught only for a local qualification) were obliged to follow an inflexible course designed for an affluent society with an infantile mortality among the lowest in Europe. Preventive medicine, social medicine, child health—the subjects obviously relevant to practice in African societies—could receive in Ibadan no more attention than was given to them in London. Even visitors from Europe pressed for some adaptation. For example, Graham Bull, a distinguished professor of medicine from Britain, wrote recently:

Expenditure should be mainly in the field of public health. Curative medicine is a luxury which must be dispensed very sparingly . . . Public opinion is still sufficiently ill informed to prefer a hospital to a piped water supply, although the latter will probably save ten times as many lives . . . British and American medical schools do not provide a suitable curriculum for doctors who are to work in Nigeria and other tropical countries . . . I was disappointed to find that University College, Ibadan, follows the British system very closely. The training it provides

* In 1947 a Yaba-trained doctor was on a salary scale of £120 rising to £400 after fifteen years' service, whereas a doctor trained in the United Kingdom was on a salary scale of £400–£720, though both might be performing exactly similar duties.

is as good as anywhere in Britain, but it is of the wrong sort. I believe that emphasis on preventive medicine should be very much greater. There is an opportunity here to develop a new approach to medicine which will be unique in providing an example for other developing countries to follow.[18]

As to more fundamental changes in the university curriculum, such as might have come from a study of the philosophy of education in African societies, there was before independence no sign whatever. This is at first surprising, for British official policy has conceded the need for adaptation in African education ever since 1925, and there have been many repetitions of the sentiments of that first White Paper. Thus in 1937 the De la Warr Commission on Higher Education in East Africa, after asking, with commendable irony, whether we should assume that European education is the most perfect yet devised, went on to hope that governments setting up a university in East Africa would "plan an educational system which will give to Africa the opportunity to fashion an indigenous culture which would be no less African because it represented a synthesis of both African and European elements."[19] And the delegation under Sir William Hamilton Fyfe which preceded the planting of university colleges in Ghana and Nigeria pressed for adaptation, even in Arts subjects. Moreover in Achimota, when it was a school, there had been some rethinking of the purpose of education and some interesting experiments based on this rethinking. Diedrich Westermann joined the staff to create a common script for Twi and Fanti. Folk tales and oral historical traditions were collected. There was encouragement of native music and drumming. There was a deliberate attempt to "produce a type of student who is 'Western' in his intellectual attitude towards life, with a respect for science and capacity for systematic thought, but who remains African in sympathy and desirous of preserving and developing what is deserving of respect in tribal life, custom, rule and law."[20]

It was inevitable that with the coming of full university education these aspirations for adapting the syllabus should be put aside in favour of more urgent, and at that time more important, aspirations. Clearly the most valuable service which the new and enthusiastic expatriate staff could perform was to establish standards in the teaching and research of subjects in which they were already experts. For the chief aspiration, quite rightly, was to reach in Africa standards of academic achievement in no way inferior to those in London: in brief, to put the African degree on the gold standard of learning. This preoccupation with uniform and high standards is, as I described earlier, a distinctive feature of British higher education. The British certainly succeeded in transferring this feature to tropical Africa. Indeed Britain's greatest gift to higher education in Africa has been to demonstrate to Africans that they can compete successfully in the European academic world. In 1960, for instance (the last year before the links with London were loosened), some 300 students in East and West Africa sat for degree examinations of the University of London. Eighty per cent of them passed. This percentage pass is about the same as that for internal candidates in the colleges of the University of London. Within ten years the university colleges in Nigeria and Ghana had earned their hall-marks of excellence. Their graduates carried away the modern equivalent of *ius ubique docendi*.

But it was unquestionably a hall-mark in the European style. This was the declared intention of some of the founders. No-one asserted it with more eloquence than the first principal of the University College of the Gold Coast in his inaugural address. He is discussing whether a university in Africa should be any different from universities anywhere else. He makes the point that the diversities between (say) historians from different universities are quite trivial compared with the diversities between (say) historians and chemists within the same university. Then he goes on to say:

> The whole issue has been bedevilled by our careless use of the phrase "European civilisation." It may be justifiable that the things which are studied at universities . . . are themselves the instruments of civilisation. If so, then it follows that there is only one modern civilisation. It happens to have started in Greece . . . and it spread first through Europe. But it is high time we stopped calling it European as though there were some other from which to distinguish it . . . I was astonished when I came here to find myself called a European. I had never thought of myself as one before, and I don't now . . .[21]

The principal admitted that within the one world-civilisation there are different national cultures, though he doubted whether universities were concerned with these or whether national cultures could (or should) be kept alive by teaching them. After all (he said) folk dancing is dying out in England and hand-looms have been replaced by machinery. "I don't think we need weep when national traditions go . . . it is only a matter of pride in superficial things."

I wonder whether these sentiments of an English classicist might be regarded as a trifle parochial by a Chinese scholar, or a Bengali, or an Arab, or even a Russian. Of course it was a sensible pragmatic decision for a university exported from Britain to concentrate on the disciplines lying within its own tradition. But to elevate this pragmatism to the dignity of a dogma, and to convey the impression that Greece is the cradle of all philosophy and Palestine the cradle of all religion is surely to speak with the voice of Macaulay and the East India Company a century ago.

Still, this is the lesson that has been taught. The Mediterranean—Africans were told—"is the cradle of all the civilisation that has conquered the world. Happy is Africa, whose shore is on that sea." And the lesson has been learnt. Until comparatively recently no African language could be studied at university level in West Africa, not even Arabic; but Latin, Greek, and the history of the Greeks and Romans were put, as Europe had put them for centuries, at the core of the humanities. In Ghana, in the session 1959–60, twelve undergraduates were devoting their *full time* to Latin, Greek, and Ancient History. In Ibadan, while the University College was in special relation with London, there were seven one-subject honours schools. Three out of the seven were in classics; and in 1961 ten students graduated in one or other of these honours schools devoted exclusively to Latin, Greek, and Ancient History. It is not, of course, only the British who have carried this particular manifestation of European cultural nationalism into African universities. The curriculum in Louvanium University in Leopoldville, for example, faithfully reflects the curriculum of Louvain in Belgium. To enter the faculty of philosophy and letters a Congolese child has to possess a *diplome homologué d'humanités gréco-latines*. Of the four options then open to him, the two most popular are *philologie roman*, where he can be seen assiduously pursuing a course which includes medieval French, equipped with stencilled extracts from the *Chanson de Roland*, and *philologie classique*, where he will have an austere and rigorous grounding in Latin and Greek. In justice to the Belgians, however, let it be said that no Congolese student, even in these courses, can avoid a broad education, including at least an introduction to African literature and history, philosophy, and psychology: a better balanced education than is offered by the honours schools at any of the English-speaking university colleges in Africa. And Louvanium offers another option in the faculty of philosophy and letters, called *philologie africaine*, which has at its core a scholarly study of African languages and cultures.

Social Function. I suppose it would be true to say that in the United States of America the predominant social function of universities was determined by the rise and success of the land grant colleges. The American university offers to the American people a great diversity of subjects and it tolerates a great spread in standards of achievement. Despite the indictments of Abraham Flexner and the protestations of Robert Maynard Hutchins, it is now pretty clear that this diversity and tolerance have given a new dimension to higher education. Particle physics and topology and African linguistics can be studied in American universities at levels not surpassed anywhere in the world. Other subjects, such as news editing and first aid, can be studied in American universities too, presumably at a more modest level. These and similar topics appear very rarely in university calendars outside the United States; but perhaps—the question is worth asking—news editing and first aid are practised at a lower level outside the United States, too. My distinguished predecessor in the Godkin Lectures gave in 1963 a spirited defence of the "multiversity." For the present I want to draw only one conclusion from the American scene. It is this. The American experience seems to me to prove conclusively that Gresham's Law does not necessarily operate in the academic world. Provided high standards have been set, "bad" degrees do not drive out "good" degrees.* Harvard awards a bachelor's degree; so does the Sharon Baptist Liberal Arts College. No-one believes that a Harvard A.B. and a Sharon A.B. represent equivalent levels of achievement. No-one believes that the Harvard A.B. is in danger of devaluation on this account.

In Britain there is an impregnable assumption that university degrees are subject to Gresham's Law; hence the scrupulous care taken to safeguard standards. The consequences of this assumption permeate many practices in British universities: the insistence on high entry standards, the preoccupation with honours degrees, the interchange of external examiners. Until the Robbins Report was published, we were only gradually growing out of the view that higher education was for a carefully selected élite. Adoption of the central axiom of the Robbins Report ("that courses of higher education should be available for all those who are qualified by ability and attainment to pursue them and who wish to do so") may persuade the British to re-examine their

---

* This assertion is not valid where high standards have never been set, as in India. There, where the degree tends to be valued more as a status symbol than as a certificate of proficiency, there is evidence that universities with lower standards tend to drag down universities which try to improve their standards.

assumptions about Gresham's Law and degrees. But through-out the 1950's, when universities were being set up in Ghana and Nigeria, in East Africa and Central Africa, the assumptions were unquestioned. The founders of these universities worked in the belief that the social function of a university in Africa was to create and sustain an intellectual élite.

What the founders could not have foreseen is the disruptive effect of this concept of higher education on African society. Even in England we have witnessed the social dilemma of the "first generation student"; Richard Hoggart's *Uses of Literacy* gives a vivid example of how a university education may drive a wedge between a young man and his working-class family. In England the side-effects of social mobility are negligible compared with their effects in Africa. For an African the impact of a university education is something inconceivable to a European. It separates him from his family and his village (though he will, with intense feeling and loyalty, return regularly to his home and accept what are often crushing family responsibilities). It obliges him to live in a Western way, whether he likes to or not. It stretches his nerve between two spiritual worlds, two systems of ethics, two horizons of thought. In his hands he holds the terrifying instrument of Western civilisation: the instrument which created Jefferson's speeches, the philosophy of Marx, the mathematics and chemistry of atomic destruction. His problem is how to apply this instrument to the welfare of his own people. But he has no opportunity to reflect on this problem. For one thing, the gap between himself and his people is very great. Moreover his degree carries him into a bewildering current of social mobility. Some of his primeval responsibilities to a traditional society remain;

at the same time new "Western" responsibilities pile up on his desk, of the kind which an equivalent graduate in Europe might not get until after twenty years' experience. He has no adequate supporting staff. His days are filled by the pressing and daunting problems of mere survival in Western society. In the United Nations, in the markets of the world, at conference tables, it is the African graduate who carries on his shoulders the destiny of his continent. The university is the nursery where he is nurtured and where his ideas are shaped. "In our time," Dr. Nkrumah once said, "the universities are looked upon almost as if they were the heart of the nation, essential to its life and progress." Yet, although they are "the heart of the nation," the universities and their graduates are isolated from the life of the common people in a way which has had no parallel in England since the middle ages. This is the peculiar dilemma of the African university. Because of this dilemma the social function of the university in Africa cannot, for a generation at least, be comparable with its social function in Britain. And the African graduate, who alone is competent to reflect on the social function of universities in Africa, has no time for this task.

III. African Nationalism Confronts the University

PUBLIC ATTITUDES

We cannot embrace the technological and reject the cultural implications of Western civilisation. We must involve ourselves in both. But in this process we are in danger of losing altogether—as the American Negro in different circumstances has lost—all sympathy with the basic culture of our society.[22]

More and more in proportion as we adopt Western manners and the Western way of life the native cultural patterns lose their sharpness . . . Are we to abandon all the values of our traditional life for those of the alien culture? . . . The best thing is . . . to try . . . to have it both ways. We must accept the *lingua franca* that history has already forced upon us but we must fight tooth and nail to preserve our own languages in all the instinctive aspects of our culture.[23]

These words come from editorials of the Lagos *Daily Times* in 1955, seven years after the University College, Ibadan, had been opened. They reflect the ambivalent public attitude of Nigerians toward the British pattern of higher education: on the one hand ambition to have institutions as similar as possible to the best to be found in Britain, on the other hand fear that these very institutions would destroy the foundations of their society and set up barriers between a Westernized élite and the mass of the people.

Ever since the university colleges opened their doors in Ghana and Nigeria, there has scarcely been a week without comment in the West African press about higher education. No detail was too trivial, no issue too technical, for the West African public; and over some issues, such as academic standards, the Africanisation of staff, the content of the curriculum, and control of universities by the state, there has been a running debate for fifteen years. To follow the course of this debate is to watch African nationalism confronting the British academic heritage. Despite differences in the temperature of politics and in the personalities playing on the intellectual stage, the debates have run on similar lines in Ghana and Nigeria and they seem to be flowing toward similar conclusions.

Academic Standards. Over standards and quality the debate is overwhelmingly in favour of preserving the British academic heritage. It is true that from time to time there are murmurs of complaint in the press (often from disgruntled contributors to the correspondence columns) about the "rigid method of selection of candidates for entrance to the University";[24] the aim in Nigeria should not be "to compete with standards of British institutions."[25] Entrance examinations should be lowered as a way to hasten Nigerianisation.[26] It has been alleged that degree standards were too high (or the teaching was inefficient), because candidates rejected by University College, Ibadan, were getting places in British or American universities and doing well; it has been protested that it is the colonial mentality which had led Nigerians to regard American degrees as "cheap."[27] The criticisms covered, too, the high standards of accommodation and the lavish expenditure on University College, Ibadan. When the Federal House of Representatives approved grants to the college in 1954, Dr. Azikiwe, speaking on the motion, said he was compelled "to denounce those whose sheer ineptitude" had brought about the overspending. The college, he said, "is becoming a million pound baby simply because it knows that whenever it cries it will be accorded a million pound kiss."[28] Oxford and Cambridge, said a speaker in the House of Representatives in 1955, did not start in the elaborate way the University College in Ibadan had started; and in order to accommodate more students, much simpler hostels should be built. The Action Group (then the principal party of Nigeria's Western Region), in its manifesto for the 1959 elections, went further still. It made much of the fact that entry to Ibadan was limited not by the size of staff or by accommodation for teaching but by the number of beds; and it vigorously advocated a departure from the principle of hundred per cent residence.[29]

All these attacks were vigorously repulsed. Over standards of admission at one end and quality of degrees at the other, neither government nor university college made any compromise, even when the flow of suitably qualified candidates diminished and there was a danger of empty beds in the college. "We don't want another Yaba" said Awokoya (Minister of Education in the Western Region)—Yaba being the forerunner of University College, Ibadan, which awarded no degrees but diplomas with only local currency. A suggestion made by several critics—that Nigeria should look to Egypt for a pattern of higher education (with easy entrance, enormous classes, nonresidential students, and teaching at night) —was rejected with contempt in the editorials of the Lagos *Daily Times*. Advocates of an American-type university met similar opposition ("Zik wants a Yank-style university at cut rates," wrote one commentator who then proceeded to defend the standards at Ibadan). An American-type university has in fact been established at Nsukka in Eastern Nigeria, partly as a response to the pressures of African nationalism for diversity in higher education; but it is indicative of Nigerian public opinion that its founder (Dr. Azikiwe) assured the public shortly before the university opened its doors that it would maintain high standards.[30] It is significant, too, that students in this new university have already become anxious about the currency of their degree and have asked the authorities for assurances that when they graduate they will not be regarded as inferior to graduates from Ibadan.

In other parts of tropical Africa public opinion about standards flowed in similar channels. In Ghana there was at first no murmur of dispute against the dedication to quality— the need to "set standards," so emphatically enunciated by the first principal, David Balme.[31] A proposal made at the college convocation as early as 1953, that the college should grant its own degrees, was rejected by a large majority with evident approval from the press, partly on the ground that an Accra degree might be considered inferior to a London degree. But murmurs did begin in 1955, when there were a hundred empty places in the University College, and the college nevertheless raised its entrance requirements "in conformity with the requirements of the University of London." For a time the press commented on the thin trickle of graduates and regretted the policy of sending down students who failed their examinations when the need for graduates was so great. The "obsession" (as the students' magazine put it) "of satisfying London examination requirements is too great for this College." And concerning agricultural education, the head of the school of agriculture at the Kumasi College of Technology wrote in 1958:

> I am convinced that since we in this country are not producing agriculturalists for any other country there is very little point in basing our course on an imaginary universal or even British standard. The whole question of standards is relative ... A standard in education is high enough when it can adequately serve the needs of the community for which it is designed. As the problems become complex so the standard must grow to deal with them.[32]

But all such criticism was summarily dismissed by the principal of the University College, and editorial comment in the press supported him. Standards, he declared (conveniently disregarding a mountain of evidence to the contrary) are "unchangeable." A new institution making its reputation "cannot afford any weakening of standards." Authority, in the person of Dr. Nkrumah, defended this declaration. Speaking after his installation as chancellor of the University of Ghana, he said that for nearly thirteen years the University College of the Gold Coast had been in special relationship with the University of London in order to ensure high standards. Adequate care had been taken to ensure that the standard of learning and scholarship which the University of Ghana had inherited was acceptable anywhere in the world. And he ended with these words: "By the attainment of University status I trust that both the lecturers and the students of the College have accepted the challenge to maintain the high academic standards already set."[33]

From East Africa comes a similar story. "It is a duty we owe to future generations" (I quote an editorial in the *Uganda Herald*) "to see they have educational facilities of a no less high standard than those we enjoy today."[34] "East Africa is fortunate in that within 50 years she has an educational institution at which her students can acquire degrees of one of the most highly considered universities in England."[35] As the University College of East Africa approached the time when it should sever its connection with London, the Uganda Minister of Education defended the admissions policy of the college, which "had never yet failed to ensure a high calibre annual intake to Makerere."[36] A few months later an editorial, discussing the proposed federal University of East Africa, declared: "It is particularly important that East Africa's own degrees shall have a standing at least comparable with the London University degrees that are now awarded."[37] Even when, in 1961, there were 50 empty places at Makerere, and when one correspondent complained that it was easier to get a degree in a British university than in East Africa, half a dozen other correspondents came to the defence of the high standards at Makerere; and a leading article in the *Uganda Argus* said concerning the new autonomous University of East Africa that it "must certainly be able to resist pressure on the maintenance of standards . . ."[38]

In Khartoum, Dakar, and Leopoldville one finds a similar climate of opinion about standards. London guaranteed and stabilised the academic standards of qualifications from Ghana, Nigeria, and the Sudan; and London's guarantee was willingly accepted and gratefully acknowledged.[39] Paris and

Bordeaux guaranteed standards in Senegal, and Senegal responded by asking, after independence, for Dakar University to be adopted as the eighteenth university of France. Louvain still guarantees standards at the university in Leopoldville. African nationalism has on the whole exerted no pressure upon the universities to cheapen their degrees.

Africanisation. Before the second world war it was possible to find occasional articles in the Australian press, headed "No Australian need apply," and listing a selection of key posts in government service and universities in Australia held by British citizens, together with their salaries. Even today the Australianisation of Australian universities is far from complete: something like forty per cent of the professorships in Australian universities are held by men who took their first degree in countries outside Australia.

I begin with this digression in order to make the point that Africanisation of the staff of universities in Africa, though one of the most delicate and sensitive points of contact between Africans and Europeans, is not merely a colour problem, and is not confined to Africa. In Africa, however, the implications of having expatriates in universities are inseparable from the emotions of African nationalism. This accounts for the conflicting currents of public opinion about Africanisation: on no topic in African academic life does what is said bear less resemblance to what is meant.

Consider first what is said. In 1953, when the University College in Accra was less than five years old, there was a debate in the Legislative Assembly calling for the replacement of various expatriates by Africans, and there has been a trickle of comment in the Ghanaian press ever since. "For over twelve years," said the Accra *Evening News,* "it was the studied policy of the British Principals who headed our institutions of higher learning to put obstacles in the way of Ghanaianisation of the teaching staff."[40] And from the Lagos *Daily Times* comes a warning that the college management should bear the word "Nigerianisation" in mind;[41] and, in an editorial, there was comment on scathing attacks made on University College, Ibadan, by those who felt that "the College was trudging the road to Nigerianisation of its academic staff with leaden feet."[42] The Nigerian Action Group manifesto of 1958 is particularly critical (though its indictment seems totally unsupported by evidence):

That the staffing policy of the College [University College, Ibadan] is influenced by colonialist consideration is again seen clearly in the system of promotions pursued by the College whereby many capable Nigerians are kept down in junior posts while expatriates of very mediocre ability are often appointed to senior posts such as senior lectureships and professorships.[43]

In East Africa the university college has until recently been free from this sort of comment. But as the sentiments of nationalism are mobilised, there has come a call from Uganda, too, to Africanise its university college. On 19 and 20 July 1963 the press reported a debate in the Uganda Parliament on a motion regretting the slow rate of Africanisation at Makerere College and urging the government to appeal to the College Council "to rectify the situation."[44]

One cannot help sympathising with those Africans who feel uneasy about the part played by expatriates in decision-making in their universities. Africa is utterly dependent on her graduates to lead their continent into the age of technology. Her universities have become, in Dr. Nkrumah's

words, the "focus of national life, reflecting the social, economic, cultural and political aspirations of the people."[45] Yet
these same universities not only insisted on being treated as
autonomous corporations, financed by the State though
claiming exemption from State control; worse than that:
decision-making on academic matters was in the hands of
senates composed almost exclusively of expatriates constantly
looking to Britain for advice and guidance. Academic and
even administrative appointments were made only after consultation with the Inter-University Council for Higher
Education—a body sitting in London and composed of
representatives of British universities. No wonder Chief
Awolowo, speaking at an Action Group Congress in Calabar
in 1958, said: "our political independence would be a sham
. . . if the control of much of our intellectual life remains in
foreign hands, and the policy of our premier University
College [he was referring to University College, Ibadan] is
decisively influenced by bodies established outside this country." And Dr. Azikiwe, in the course of a Foundation Day
ceremony at Ibadan in 1961, declared: "There is no need for
us to be running helter-skelter abroad begging for experts to
come and guide us when we have indigenous experts galore
in Nigeria." Unfortunately there are not indigenous experts
galore in Nigeria, nor will there be for a generation yet. But
we must not expect this indigestible fact to bring comfort to
Africans. They inevitably feel as Americans would feel in
Cambridge, Massachusetts, if sixty per cent of their faculty
were British; or we would feel in Cambridge, England, if
sixty per cent of our dons were American.

So much for what is said. But it is not consistent with what
is meant. Foreign experts, if they come in the right spirit, are

welcomed in tropical Africa. African leaders, speaking in private, are frank in their appeals to Europeans to come to Africa to teach, to build roads, to provide the skills of accountants, quantity surveyors, statisticians, and the like. Africans display to the expatriate who comes to serve them an urbane courtesy and a thoughtful hospitality; they openly seek his advice; they are receptive even to his adverse criticism. Quite properly, they want to reserve to themselves responsibility for policy-making in their own country. For this reason they want to have Africans in posts where important policy decisions have to be made; but, even in many of these posts, they do not want to exclude expatriates at the expense of quality or efficiency. In one African university college the story is told of an expatriate college principal who announced to his governing body that if there were two candidates for a professorship, one European and the other African and both able to fill the post, he would recommend the African without considering further which of the two candidates was the better one. Whereupon the African members of the governing body protested that this was not the way to maintain academic standards and to build up a good institution. And there have been other instances when British advisers have urged African governments to fill some key post or other with an African, only to be told that "for the present" the African government preferred to have the services of an expatriate.

It is always risky for a European to interpret African opinion. But I shall take the risk and give you my personal view over the question of Africanisation: it is this. The humiliations of colonialism cut deep, especially the implicit, if not explicit, job-reservation which used to be practised in the colonies, whereby Africans were eligible only for posts in the lower ranks of the professions. The educational system in the colonies up to the outbreak of the second world war reflected this policy. In Nigeria, for instance, the only institution for post-secondary education—Yaba Higher College —regulated its entry according to manpower demands for its diplomates; and the diplomates were never able to command the salaries or the status of university graduates. Moreover, there were different salary scales for Africans and expatriates with similar qualifications doing similar work. Of course, compared with other European powers in Africa—especially Belgium and Portugal and South Africa—the British policy on the employment of Africans was liberal and enlightened; but, even a dozen years ago, there still persisted a discrimination which exasperated educated Africans. So in the new states of Africa official policy, public statement, the party line, have to be for the replacement of all expatriates in responsible posts by Africans. But most African leaders are far too intelligent and anxious for their people to acquire the techniques of the West, to allow this policy to stand in the way of progress. They can distinguish easily enough the European who is in Africa for what he can get out of it—or who comes with the paternalistic attitude of a neocolonialist —from the European who is in Africa because he likes Africans and wants to serve them and to learn about their problems. As with so much else in Africa, what is done over Africanisation is much more important that what is said.

Content of Curriculum. With regard to the content of university courses, public attitudes have grown into a consistent pressure upon the imported traditions of European academic life. It was widely accepted that during the initial phase, while tropical Africa established itself on the gold standard of learning, the content of higher education could not vary except in trivial detail from that in the metropolitan country. But it was not long before this sensible and reasonable pragmatism became the subject of heated debate, a debate which still goes on, with enthusiasts for the European tradition (including many Africans) entrenched in defensive positions and enthusiasts for African cultural nationalism (including some Europeans) attacking their positions. As with the "Asquith doctrine," so with the content of curricula: a policy which began as a convenient working hypothesis became for some people petrified into a dogma. Dogmas are liable to be defended with emotion rather than with reason. And this, of course, means that dogmas are liable to be attacked, too, with emotion rather than with reason. As in so many disputes between intellectuals, arguments based on pedantry, prejudice, and vague abstract principles carry more weight than arguments based on common sense and the pragmatic approach.

Let us try to unravel the complexities of the debate. Everyone on both sides was prepared to agree that subjects such as mathematics and physics could not be taught any differently just because the students belonged to a Hamitic race living in latitude 10° and not to a Nordic race living in latitude 50°. Everyone was prepared to agree that details of the syllabus in such subjects as biology, geography, and history should be modified to make the subjects more relevant to African conditions. The link with the University of London set no restraint upon the African colleges over these modifications in detail: indeed, some of the more progressive academics in

London complained that the African colleges had not availed themselves sufficiently of the flexibility which London permitted.[46]

The points of difference were much more fundamental than these. African nationalism challenged the European tradition over the very purpose of the university in Africa. Is it true (as David Balme so eloquently assured the people of Ghana) that there is only one kind of university, concerned with only one tradition of learning? Or should the universities of Africa refurnish the house of Western tradition and adapt their degree structure to fit the needs of African society? When a Ghanaian Minister of State, Kojo Botsio, cautiously suggested at a conference in 1955 that African universities should adapt their curricula to the present needs of Africa and at the same time preserve the best from the university systems of Europe and America, the rejoinder was that all an African university needed to do was to follow the European tradition: "that was what every country outside Europe had done . . ."[47]

If Africans had never studied in the United States they might have acquiesced in this dogmatic fidelity to the European tradition. But many Africans, including such leaders as Azikiwe and Nkrumah, were familiar with American universities. There they saw that European academic tradition had undergone massive adaptations, and in directions, too, which seemed appropriate for Africa.

It is instructive to compare the Ph.D. theses of Africans who have done research on education in London and in New York. A period of study in Britain frequently consolidates in an African a respect for the British educational system. A period of study in America frequently nurtures a dissatisfaction with the British system—not always, perhaps, for very profound reasons. U. Okeke, for instance[48] writes in his Ph.D. thesis that he saw a peculiar relevance in the pattern of American education, for this pattern was worked out while America was a colony fighting to gain its independence. Therefore the history of American education is a valuable tool "in the hands of colonials struggling to obtain their freedom from alien rule." Okeke was impatient with British gradualism: "the British were in Nigeria for many years before the ascendancy of the U.S.S.R., the modernisation of Japan, the revival of Turkey"; yet, apart from the endeavours of Christian missionaries, nothing until recently was achieved in Nigerian education. Another African Ph.D. student in New York—as long ago as 1946—was impressed by the relevance of American education to the needs of American society and he wrote, "The ideal of adapting education to local environment is contradicted by the octopus of British-sponsored external examinations . . . One of the strongest charges that could be made against education in Nigeria and one around which all other charges revolve, is that it lacks adaptation."[49]

Pressure for adaptation, as judged from press comment and speeches in parliament, increased continually over the years 1948–1963. It took two common forms: complaints that priorities in the curriculum were out of phase with Africa's needs for high-level manpower, and complaints that the curriculum was not putting down roots into indigenous African culture.

The first form of complaint is well summarised in the manifesto on higher education issued by the Action Group in 1958. University College, Ibadan, the manifesto said, had at that time no courses in engineering, economics, law, geology, anthropology, sociology, public administration, or Arabic and Islamic studies, and had taken eight years to establish a department of education. Yet there were courses in Christian religious knowledge (with a staff of three), and also in Latin, Greek, and Ancient History. As evidence for the demand for the missing fields of study the manifesto asserted that in 1956 there were 986 Nigerians in Britain studying engineering, economics, or law. Furthermore, the whole emphasis within science was on pure science, at a time when West Africa's needs were predominantly in applied science and technology. A similar policy was being pursued in Accra: theoretical teaching and fundamental research were given the first priority: applied science, urgently needed for the development of the country, had to find its first home elsewhere.

The source of this policy lay in England, for these attitudes to applied science were forced upon Ibadan and Accra by the decision, made in London, to put engineering training in West Africa into the colleges of arts, science and technology (one at Kumasi and one at Zaria). But public resentment—that applied science, West Africa's prime need, should be relegated to colleges below university status—was none the less justified. The idea that universities in tropical Africa might recapitulate the phylogeny of universities in Europe, and begin (as universities in Salerno and Bologna began) as societies primarily concerned with vocational training in technologies and professions, was not part of the "Asquith doctrine." If it had been, one might have seen in British West Africa a fresh and totally different pattern of higher education, with agriculture, engineering, economics, medicine, and teacher training at the core of the curriculum; and "pure scholarship" in science and the humanities arising as natural consequences of these vocational studies. There was an opportunity to do for Africa in the 1960's what the Morrill Act did for America in the 1860's, namely to make a new contribution to the idea of a university. But the Asquith Commission took no account of American experience.

By the early and middle 1950's the Ghana press was asking for facilities for training accountants, bankers, and business managers,[50] and for greater emphasis on vocational training.[51] Warnings of the need for adaptation came also from the highest levels. As early as 1954, Dr. Nkrumah was reported as saying: "While I fully subscribe to the vital principle of academic freedom, a University must relate its activities to the needs of the society in which it exists . . ."[52] And Dr. Azikiwe turned his views on this matter into action, by creating at Nsukka, in Nigeria, a new university to operate on the lines of an American land grant college, with its emphasis on vocational training. "We cannot afford," he said, "to continue to produce . . . an upper class of parasites who shall prey upon a stagnant and sterile class of workers and peasants . . . We must frankly admit that we can no longer afford to flood only the white collar jobs at the expense of the basic occupations and productive vocations . . . particularly in the fields of agriculture, engineering, business administration, education and domestic science."[53]

One manifestation of African nationalism, then, was to bring to bear upon the universities a pressure for relevance to the short-term needs of African society: a curriculum which should be empirical, down-to-earth, and calculated to diminish the menacing gap which existed—and still exists—between the intellectuals and the mass of the people. There was an impatience with the British traditions of clerkly and literary education. There was unease that higher, and even secondary, education was disrupting the stability of African society by alienating Africans from the core of their culture: the land, the village, the family. Must education be destructive? "It seems ironical," wrote one observer, "that the Nigerian community is approaching the point at which every child allowed to proceed to secondary school becomes a liability, not only in his unproductiveness, but also in his demand from society for a place he does not merit."[54] Gradually public opinion crystallised into a demand that a university in Africa should serve the needs of the State for expertise and high-level manpower. Public opinion was not content to see reproduced in the African bush a replica of a traditional European temple of learning, although this was the very policy which had, a dozen years earlier, given Africans confidence in themselves. Scores of times the taunt of "ivory tower" was thrown at the university colleges in Ghana and Nigeria.

At the same time the pressure of African nationalism upon the curriculum is manifested in another and quite different form. There is a desire to see the incorporation into the undergraduate course of material about the indigenous cultures of tropical Africa: its traditional political systems, with their subtle checks and balances; its passionate identification with the soil through religion, customary law, the cultivation of crops and the care of animals; its philosophies and codes of behaviour; its languages; its folklore and music and dance.

Until very recently (it is still true in the University of Ibadan) an African could graduate even in the humanities in utter ignorance of the roots of his own heritage. And this knowledge is not simply of antiquarian interest. A teacher who does not understand or respect the village culture of his pupils cannot reach their minds. An administrator unfamiliar with the customs of the people in his charge cannot earn their confidence. A lawyer, a doctor, an engineer, who is out of touch with the society he serves, cannot serve that society well.

Ever since higher education was brought to West Africa, public opinion has fumbled its way toward these conclusions. Editorials in the Lagos newspapers pleaded for a study of the vernacular languages (before independence none of these could be studied in any English-speaking university in tropical Africa) and for the promotion of an indigenous African literature.[55] As long ago as 1955 the editorial column of the Lagos *Daily Times* was advocating a faculty of Nigerian languages at Ibadan,[56] and in 1956, again in an editorial, there was a plea that Arabic should be taught there.[57]

In Ghana the famous Achimota College, as early as 1927, set an admirable precedent for the study of African indigenous languages and culture, and one of David Balme's early decisions as first principal of the University College at Accra was to institute a research school of African Studies there. In 1951 a columnist in the Accra *Daily Graphic* was asking whether higher education "should be related to local histories, traditions and environment"—and he answered his own question by pointing to the "cultural renaissance" already at that time evident in the Gold Coast. And Dr.

Nkrumah, when he opened Akuafo Hall of Residence at the University College in February 1956, made his policy clear: "We must in the development of our University bear in mind that once it had been planted in African soil it must take root amidst African traditions and culture."[58]

Of course there has been opposition to these two manifestations of the pressure of African nationalism on the curriculum. Although Africa's prime need from its universities is for the broadly educated citizen capable of manning the civil service and the schools, and for general practitioners in the professions, rather than for research-minded specialists who have concentrated upon one-subject honours courses, the aspirations of individual expatriate professors and the determination of Africans to ape practice in England have conspired to keep courses too narrow and too much oriented to research. Some African intellectuals, especially those educated in Britain, resist changes in curriculum or in pattern of courses because they confuse such changes with a lowering of standards. They are accordingly suspicious of any divergence from the British pattern. Some of them are particularly allergic to proposals for incorporating African studies into the curriculum. Is this, they say, the first step toward disarming us intellectually; to substitute Arabic and African languages for the classics; to teach English to Africans as Chinese is taught to Englishmen, not as Englishmen learn English at Cambridge; to neglect Tudor history in favour of the history of Africa; to regard oral tradition as legitimate material for scholarship; to take seriously the political institutions of a Yoruba town; to reflect on the indigenous ethical systems of animists and Moslems as well as on

Christian ethics? This resistance to adaptation on the part of some African intellectuals is supported by a few—but by no means all—of the expatriates who still dominate academic policy-making in tropical Africa.

There are, of course, sound reasons for caution. To teach African studies at undergraduate level is a much harder task than to teach European or Middle Eastern or Russian studies. The subject is not codified. The documents are incomplete. The textbooks are not yet written. But these arguments are used disingenuously by those who are afraid of adaptation; it is evident from the curricula in *philologie Africaine* at Leopoldville and in *sociologie musulmane africaine* and *linguistique africaine* at Dakar that the subject can be taught—and is already being taught to French-speaking Africans—in a scholarly way at undergraduate level and with no softening of standards. Indeed, individual departments in English-speaking colleges have already demonstrated this. For example, the Department of Religious Studies in University College, Ibadan, for years offered a scholarly course on African religions, including lectures on witchcraft.

Notwithstanding some resistance, the two pressures—the one for a greater proportion of vocational training relevant to Africa's needs, the other for the incorporation of a study of indigenous cultures into the curriculum—have already evoked a lively response from the universities in Ghana and Nigeria. In Ghana there was a landslide of opinion when the State decided to intervene in university policy. In both of the newly created universities—the University of Ghana, near Accra, and the Kwame Nkrumah University, in Kumasi—striking changes were made in the curriculum. It was an-

nounced in October 1961 that the Institute of African Studies
in the University of Ghana would be expanded and that all
undergraduates would follow in their first year a course in
African studies "stressing the unity of the African continent
in all its aspects."[59] In addition there is in Ghana a two-year
postgraduate course leading to a master's degree in African
Studies, which includes languages; history; social, political,
and economic institutions; music and art. "For the first time
since Ghana's contact with Europe in the fifteenth century,"
said one of the intellectual leaders of Ghana, recently, "the
two universities [in Ghana] are serving as places where creative and conscious reflections on life in Africa are being
undertaken."[60] For those who still doubted whether these
studies have a place in a university curriculum, the present
vice-chancellor of the University of Ghana, Conor Cruise
O'Brien, had this to say:

We should be very clear . . . that this tendency [to develop
the Institute of African Studies] is not a restrictive one . . . Far
from being a restriction, the development of interest in African
Studies is a liberation: it is a liberation from that older and nar-
rower concept of a university in Africa as being a place whose
main and virtually sole function was to pursue European studies
and disseminate European knowledge in Africa . . . In transcend-
ing that narrow concept and in becoming more fully a part of its
environment, an African university becomes not merely more
fully African but also more fully a university.[61]

The only danger in this enthusiasm for African Studies
(and I do not believe that scholars are likely to succumb to
this danger) is that it might lead to a sort of Celtic revival of

African culture investing Africa's past in a luminous mist, to airy and undisciplined talk about the great empires of Ghana and the Sudan, which could easily lead to the injection of romance, if not falsification, into history. For (as Conor Cruise O'Brien is reported to have said recently) Africa's history will be written anew by Africans. Time is needed for a distinctively African historiography to emerge, distinctive not in techniques and standards but in assumptions and interests. The questions which occur to the European in Africa have been put and have been answered in a European way. The African interests, the African assumptions, the African questions, have now to make themselves felt and the history of Africa will be written in a new way.[62] This is all very well, provided the history is written by historians and not by politicians; for some Ghanaian politicians start from the assumption that history written by Europeans must be wrong because (in the words of one of them) it contains "miscalculated information created by colonialists."

Adaptation in Ghana to the other pressure for change—the encouragement of applied science and technology—has taken the form of the elevation of the College of Arts, Science and Technology to university status as the Kwame Nkrumah University of Science and Technology. At his installation as chancellor of this university Nkrumah said: "The ivory tower concept of the University is dead (and may it rest in peace) . . . Everything will be done to place a premium on the study of science and technology."[63]

In Nigeria the impact of African nationalism upon the curriculum has been less traumatic, less dictatorial, less coloured by politics. There are two reasons for this: one is that in Nigeria faith in democracy and change by consent still govern the relations between universities and the State; the other is that the pressures of public opinion for adaptation of the curriculum were released into four new universities, leaving the original institution at Ibadan under far less duress than it might otherwise have been exposed to.

The "new look" in Nigerian universities is to be found at Nsukka in the Eastern Region. It had long been Dr. Azikiwe's belief that the American land grant college provided a better model than the British university for Nigerian higher eduction. He was impressed by its willingness to include vocational subjects, such as accountancy and journalism; its rejection of the idea that universities were to be confined to an intellectual élite; its commitment to extension work; its emphasis on farming and all that is involved in rural life. Accordingly Dr. Azikiwe founded an institution which he called the University of Nigeria, inspired by the land grant philosophy and fostered by Michigan State University. This new university was set up by law in 1955; its Provisional Council was appointed in 1959; it opened its doors in October 1960. By 1963, three years later, the university had 1,244 students and 221 members of the academic staff.

Azikiwe's university (he was installed as its executive life chancellor in 1961) has brought a refreshing diversity to higher education in Nigeria. The traditionalists in higher education, that is to say those who imagine that any departure from the "Asquith doctrine" is heresy, lost no time in deciding that the University of Nigeria would debase academic standards, for it admits many of its students after a lower level of achievement at secondary school.* But it keeps those who enter at this lower level for four years instead of three before they are eligible to take degrees, and it is too soon to say how its graduates will compare with those from Ibadan. In place of the specialisation already to be found in the sixth-form courses at secondary schools, the University of Nigeria offers a year's course in general studies, including English language and literature, social science, natural science, and the humanities. Thereafter follow in the prospectus —in true American style—literally hundreds of credit-earning courses covering the whole spectrum of knowledge from subjects as esoteric as The Rise and Fall of the Ottoman Empire (3 credits), Igbo Phonology and Morphology (2 credits), Advanced Tectonics (4 credits), Vector Analysis (9 credits), and Ethnomusicology—including Eskimo music (2 credits); to subjects as down-to-earth as Seed Testing (4 credits), Insurance (3 credits), Woodwork (9 credits), Household Sanitation (2 credits), Planning and Serving of Meals

---

* The British educational system is punctuated by public examinations. Unless a pupil is educated in a private school, his admission to a secondary school whose curriculum leads to a university depends upon his passing the so-called "Eleven-plus" (though many education authorities have now lost faith in this examination and are using alternative methods of selection). After four or five years at secondary school the pupil takes General Certificate of Education, ordinary level, or in Africa an approximately equivalent examination, the School Certificate. He then goes (if he passes) into the Sixth Form where he works for General Certificate of Education, advanced level, or in Africa its approximate equivalent, the Higher Certificate. This in Africa takes two years, and is confined to (say) three subjects. The University of Nigeria in 1961 took 30–40 per cent of its freshmen after O-level G.C.E.; and in 1962 it took 50–60 per cent after O-level. The normal entry to other Nigerian, and all British, universities, is after A-level, but American universities are accepting African students after O-level.

(4 credits); Shorthand (9 credits); and Techniques of Dancing (3 credits). The conservatives—African graduates of British universities—shake their heads reproachfully at this exuberance. They cannot conceive how the serious business of a university can be conducted in such a supermarket of education (notwithstanding the fact that other, not entirely dissimilar supermarkets in the United States, have their Nobel Prizewinners and their Members of the National Academy). I believe it is far too early for head-shaking. Only time will show whether the University of Nigeria is a viable adaptation of higher education to African needs. A Nsukka graduate, with his 192 "credit-hours" and his minimum "quality-point-average" of 2, may yet find he has as much to offer the new Nigeria as his brother-graduate from Ibadan has to offer with a three-year Arts course which may have been devoted entirely to Latin, Greek, and Ancient History of the Mediterranean, or to English literature, drama, and the literary criticism of Dr. Leavis.

As for the other institutions of higher education in Nigeria, founded in the flood tide of African cultural nationalism, Lagos University proposes to concentrate on medicine, engineering, law, and business administration; it has evening courses for adult students; and all its undergraduates have to take a course either in the problems of a changing African society, or in the biology of Man. The University of Ife, established largely to satisfy the cultural aspirations of the Western Region, is conducting evening classes and doing useful work especially in agricultural extension. The Ahmadu Bello University is already a national centre for engineering and public administration, and will become one for Islamic studies and veterinary science.

The University of Ibadan remains somewhat aloof from its younger sisters and conceives it to be its mission to put special emphasis on its research and postgraduate work. It has responded to one of the pressures of African public opinion by setting up a very promising research institute in African Studies and it has for years been the centre for distinguished work in African history and antiquities. The quality of its undergraduate teaching remains high, but even though Ibadan now has cut its ties with the University of London, there has —in the Faculty of Arts, at any rate—been virtually no adaptation in the curriculum or structure of the degree to the educational needs of the nation. Once the university was released from the control of the University of London, the two most obvious changes it might have been expected to make in its Arts curriculum were to broaden its courses to diminish specialisation (for the rank and file of students, at any rate) and to introduce for all undergraduates some material bearing on indigenous African culture and institutions. To judge from its latest prospectus (1964–65) the Faculty of Arts has admitted neither of these changes. The three-year course for the B.A. in Arts (whether ending in an honours or pass degree—there is no difference in curriculum) requires three subjects in the first year, but ties all students to a choice of only *one* school for the remaining two years (single honours) or to a choice of one of six combinations of two schools (double honours). Four of the six combinations require a classical language, Greek or Latin. The six combinations in the 1964–65 prospectus are: Biblical and English Literature, Latin and English, Greek and Religious Studies, French and Latin, French and English, Latin and Religious Studies. A student who is perverse enough not to care for any of these combinations is obliged to devote his last two years exclusively to one (and only one) of the following schools: Latin, Classics, English, History, Geography, Religious studies, Arabic and Islamic studies, Mathematics. According to the information issued to new students by the Department of Classics it is still possible for a student to graduate in Arts at Ibadan without having pursued any subjects at the university except Latin, Greek, and Greek and Roman Culture. This alone, though inviting criticism, not to say ridicule, from Africans struggling with the staggering problems of Nigeria's economy, might be dismissed as a quaint anachronism, for no student is obliged to immerse himself exclusively in these abstract and scholarly pursuits, and it is quite proper to have classics as one ingredient of a liberal education. What is much more serious is that it is *not* possible for a student who graduates in Arts to devote any substantial time in his last two years to any subject bearing on the languages or cultures of his own continent (apart from casual and incidental lectures and a welcome emphasis given to Africa in his courses in geography or history), unless he elects to read Arabic and Islamic studies: an option which is not likely to be taken except by Moslems.[64]

It is a pity that this pedantic acquiescence in a pattern of education venerable in itself but already abandoned by the new universities of Britain should have prevented any imaginative adaptation of the humanities to the African intellectual climate. As the Research Institute of African Studies grows in confidence, and as more Africans have a hand in determining academic policy in Ibadan, this obscurantist attitude to the content of the Arts degree will doubtless change. One hopes so; for Ibadan, secure in the quality of its scholarship, free from the political constraints which hamper the University of Ghana and the ecclesiastical discipline which permeates Louvanium University, could take a lead in adapting the European cultural tradition to African soil.

UNIVERSITIES AND THE STATE

Higher education in Africa confronts the aspirations of African nationalism over academic standards, where the European legacy is willingly accepted; over the replacement of expatriates by Africans, where, notwithstanding public clamour, Africans are for the present prepared to welcome expatriate teachers and research workers and do not complain provided administrative posts are Africanised; and over the content of curriculum, where some adaptations to the pressures of public opinion are already discernible. But it is over the relations between universities and governments that one would expect the most powerful pressures of African nationalism upon higher education to operate. Let us now turn to consider these relations.

African political leaders are puzzled by the uncompromising and sometimes querulous defence of university autonomy displayed on the least provocation by expatriates in the English-speaking universities of tropical Africa. For Britain is anomalous in that her universities are financed by the State and yet are established as corporations independent of the State, and it is this anomaly which has been exported to Africa. The universities of France, Germany, Sweden, and the land grant universities of America manage (with occasional lapses, it is true) to maintain traditions of academic freedom although they are frankly organs of the State; only in Britain and countries which have imported their universities from Britain do the constitutions of universities deliberately confer immunity from day-to-day State control; and only in Britain and these countries is it assumed that constitutions of this pattern are essential for preserving academic freedom. What is sometimes overlooked in Africa is that in Europe—even in Britain—and in America it is the conventions, not the constitutions, of university government which provide the real safeguards for academic freedom. There is one set of conventions for the State universities of Germany and Belgium, another for the centralised university system of France, another for the American land grant university, and another for the British civic university. When universities are exported, these conventions are unlikely to be exported with them; and this has been the cause of some difficulties in the universities of tropical Africa.

I have already described how the English-speaking universities of Africa were endowed with constitutions on the British pattern, constitutions which are peculiarly part of the British (rather than the European) academic tradition. Let us now examine how these constitutions are standing up to the pressures of African politics.

Ibadan. It is important to recollect that Africans played very little part in designing the constitutions of their first university colleges. The first draft of an ordinance for University College, Ibadan, for example, was submitted by the first principal (an Englishman) to the executive committee of the British Inter-University Council for Higher Education, in London, in 1950. The committee considered the draft inadequate. Sixteen months later the constitution—this time a new draft—was still being considered by the committee in London, and comments on it were being sent out to Nigeria. In June 1952, Sir David Hughes Parry (a distinguished lawyer and at one time vice-chancellor of the University of London) produced what became, with one major and a few minor amendments, the final draft. It was of course discussed by the infant University College itself and by the colonial government in Nigeria, but it was essentially "made in Britain." The major amendment came from the Council of Ministers in Lagos: it provided for a statutory body comprising the whole academic and administrative staff, with the duty of meeting once a year. The purpose of this body, called Congregation, was to foster the idea that this new university college, set down in the African bush, was a self-governing academic society. Apart from this wise provision, the constitution of the University College, established in March 1954, was created, discussed, and drafted in London.[65]

In 1960, after Nigerian independence, the University College prepared itself for metamorphosis into an autonomous university. A new constitution had to be drafted. The predominantly expatriate and professorial Senate proceeded on traditional British lines. They prepared a draft constitution: traditional, not to say backward looking; almost a facsimile of the charter and statutes of an English civic university of the 1940's; indeed giving sovereignty to a predominantly lay governing body, but the sort of sovereignty which cannot be exercised over academic questions except on the recommendation of a Senate which was virtually an oligarchy of professors. (At this time, 1961–62, the Senate consisted

of the Nigerian principal and twenty-nine members, twenty
of whom were professors and only five of whom were
Africans.) The draft after much discussion both by the
Senate and the College Council was approved for trans-
mission to the Parliamentary draughtsman in Lagos.

Here trouble began. The chairman of the College Council,
an African whose interests brought him close to politics,
disliked the new constitution. He expressed his misgivings
at the meeting of the Council which approved the draft, on
the grounds that the new university would be a state university and that its constitution and policies should reflect
the aspirations of the Federal Government; and he warned
the Council that the government would make any alterations
in the draft constitution it wished or deemed necessary,
notwithstanding the recommendations of the Council. He
then prepared a memorandum for the Federal Minister of
Education and the Attorney General, which set out clearly
what in his opinion (after consultation with the Visitor,
who was the Governor General of Nigeria, Dr. Azikiwe)
the federal government's policy touching university constitutions ought to be.

This memorandum is a vivid example of one feature of
the confrontation of African nationalism and the British
academic tradition. After explaining how in British civic
universities the powers vested in the Senate are almost totali-
tarian, the memorandum goes on to point out how in the
Nigerian context the senior members of the academic staff
who constitute the Senate should devote their full time to
scholarship and research. Academic freedom, says the memorandum, can be safeguarded without burdening the Senate

with executive and administrative responsibilities; these responsibilities should not be the concern of academics in a modern university. Consequently the control of policy should be vested in a Council, the majority of whose members are appointed by the State. The memorandum declares that universities in Nigeria can no longer follow the pattern of the former suzerain of a colonial Nigeria, nor can the university Senate any longer be used as an instrument for controlling the higher education of colonial peoples. In conformity to the above principles the memorandum went on to ask for a dozen major changes to be made in the draft constitution, notwithstanding the fact that the draft had been prepared by the college with meticulous care, agreed by its Council, and submitted to the federal government for legislation. The changes, if adopted, would have established the Governor-General (Dr. Azikiwe) as chancellor, with power to appoint the vice-chancellor (who is the full-time executive head of the university); given the Council, subject to the approval of the chancellor, power to terminate the appointment of the vice-chancellor "for adequate cause;" cut down the Senate representation on the Council from four to two; rejected the proposal that Congregation (the whole academic staff) should have two representatives on Council, and that Convocation (the whole body of graduates) should have one; and withdrawn the power of Council to co-opt members. This would have produced a Council of sixteen, one of whom would have been the Governor General, two of whom would have been his appointees, and nine of whom would have been the appointees of federal and regional governments. Furthermore the memorandum proposed changes which would have removed from the

Council power to appoint the chancellor and vice-chancellor and its own vice-chairman.

Had this been known at the time to the academic staff at Ibadan, there would have been a great outcry. But in fact the proposals, though shocking, were within the letter of the law, for according to the ordinance the Visitor can take what steps he likes to ensure the fulfilment of the objects of the college, and to this end the Chairman of the Council would be obliged to take instructions from him. What had been flagrantly transgressed by the Chairman of the Council was not a law, but a convention. British universities simply could not work their constitutions if this convention were disregarded.

Through the early months of 1962 the fate of the draft constitution remained in suspense. But in the end the federal government rejected the changes proposed in the memorandum from the Chairman of the College Council and adopted (with minor changes and improvements proposed by its advisers) the draft approved by the University College.[66] Over this incident, as over academic standards, African opinion (personified by the federal government) was willing to adhere to British tradition.

Ahmadu Bello, Ife, and Lagos. In Ibadan pressures to change the constitutional pattern of the University were up against a strongly fortified defence, in an institution of high prestige. But even where there was no built-in resistance to change, the conventional British model of constitution was adopted; this happened in three of the new universities: Ahmadu Bello in the Northern Region, Ife in the Western Region, and Lagos. These universities are all autonomous corporations, with two-tier government (a predominantly lay Council and a predominantly professorial Senate or Academic Board.)

The Ahmadu Bello University adopted, again with minor changes, a constitution drawn up by a working party under the chairmanship of Sir Alexander Carr-Saunders, who had been a member of the commission which created the "Asquith doctrine."[67]

The University of Ife has a provisional constitution which, although unsatisfactory in several ways (it has, for instance, quite inadequate representation of academics on the governing body, and of nonprofessorial academics on the Academic Board), still preserves a shape reminiscent of that in a prewar British civic university.[68]

The University of Lagos might easily have found itself saddled with a disastrous constitution; for the university was set up after advice had been taken from a UNESCO commission with the customary international membership.[69] This commission emphasised the need for the university to be autonomous, and then proceeded to propose a constitution which would have made autonomy impracticable: a governing body with no powers of co-option and no academic representative except the vice-chancellor; a secretary who was to be a civil servant from the Ministry of Education, nominated by the Minister; and an astonishing section entitled "Directions by the Minister" and beginning: "The Minister may give directions of a general character to the Council with respect to matters falling within the external relationships of the University . . . " (The draft goes on to say that these directions shall not be valid if they "shall be liable to conflict with the academic autonomy of the University"; but anyone familiar with academic politics knows how worthless this sort of proviso is likely to be.)

The draft constitution offered to the University of Lagos by the UNESCO commission was a sort of anthology of fragments from British and Continental university procedure. To attempt to run a university on these lines would have been like asking a mechanic to construct a car from a mixture of components, some from Ford and some from Volkswagen. Mercifully the advice of the commission on the constitution was not followed; and the university has been set up with a provisional form of government which, if conventions are followed, is adequate to ensure autonomy, except in one respect: the Medical School, for political reasons, has been established as a separate corporation under the Minister of Health. Although medical students are reading for degrees of the University of Lagos, the university has no control over admission standards, curriculum, or the appointment of staff. This anomaly does not represent enlightened opinion in Nigeria; it has already been condemned by the Nigerian Universities Commission.

From the examples I have cited so far it might be concluded that African nationalism is prepared to concede to African universities the formal detachment from the State and the statutory protection from the cross-winds of politics which are the peculiar privileges of universities in Britain. Certainly a significant section of African opinion would resist the idea that African universities should become instruments of politics. For example, when David Balme, the pioneer principal of the University College in Accra, retired in 1956, the editorial in the Accra *Daily Graphic* ran: "One of the greatest services rendered by Mr. Balme is the fact that, throughout the rapid political changes that have taken place in this country, he has never swerved from his determination that the University College should remain independent."[70] But it would be wrong to conclude that the relations between universities and states in tropical Africa will remain unaffected by the pressures of African nationalism. For years African leaders have given assurances that they would respect academic freedom, *but* . . . ; and they then go on to define (often very shrewdly and often after much reflection) what they consider to be the limitations of academic freedom in the social climate of Africa. Dr. Nkrumah, for instance, in a speech at the University of Ghana in February 1963, spoke of the necessity for a university "to maintain that honesty and objectivity which are the only keys to progress." And he assured the audience of his "readiness to defend at all times this right of the university." Then he said, "There is, however, sometimes a tendency to use the words 'academic freedom' in another sense, and to assert the claim that a university is more or less an institution of learning having no respect or allegiance to the community or to the country in which it exists . . . This assertion is unsound in principle and objectionable in practice."[71]

The Action Group policy for higher education in Nigeria, published in 1958, is less decorous in its comment. Under the subtitle "The Myth of Academic Autonomy" it asserts that "it is well known that institutions of higher education all over the world are meant to reflect, and generally do reflect, the national aspirations and needs of the countries in which they are situated . . . The community makes known its demands and the University merely supplies the demands."[72] This of course is mere political flatulence; but it would be very surprising if the British tradition of autonomy in universities, any more than the British tradition of democratic government, were to be viable in Africa without adaptation. It is therefore important to study sympathetically any departure in Africa from the English pattern of university constitution which can be attributed to the influence of African nationalism. Two such departures have been made: one in Nigeria and one in Ghana. They constitute instructive case histories in adaptation.

University of Nigeria. This is the university founded by Dr. Azikiwe after the pattern of an American land grant college. Its history begins in 1955 with the enactment of the University of Nigeria Law, 1955, in the Eastern Region, which established on paper what was in fact the first institution of full university status in Nigeria;[73] but only on paper, for it was another five years before the university opened its doors to students. The act can be taken to represent what was in 1955 a contemporary African point of view; it had no need to be consistent with British traditions of university government nor to be constrained by British colonial policy. So far as is known, those who framed the act were innocent of any formal advice from the Inter-University Council in London, the body whose views were normally sought before the creation of university colleges in British colonial territories. Moreover it was well known that one of the aspirations of the founder of the new university was to break away from the British tradition and to adopt some features of the American land grant college. One might therefore have expected in the act a pattern of government reminiscent of Wisconsin or Iowa or Kansas. In fact, however, the provisions for Council, Senate, and faculties follow almost word for word the 1954 ordinance of University College, Ibadan. The only noteworthy divergences from this very English constitution were (a) appointment of three Visitors (all from the Eastern Region: the Governor, the Premier, and the Minister of Education) in place of one; (b) greater representation on the Council from the Eastern Region than from other regions, at the expense of representation from the Senate; (c) provision for twenty "institutes," vague in function and miscellaneous in coverage, including architecture, domestic science, dramatics, journalism, music, physical education, public health, and secretarial studies; and (d) the appointment of deans of faculties by the Council instead of by the faculty boards. The first two divergencies indicated that despite its embracing title, the new university was to be a regional rather than a federal institution. The third divergence—the twenty "institutes"—represented a step toward diversifying higher education and departing from the conventional diet offered by Ibadan. The fourth divergence —appointment of deans by the Council—was a straw which showed that the wind of African academic politics was veering toward a more hierarchical and a less democratic quarter. But these divergencies were comparatively trivial: the significant fact is that in the 1955 law the constitutional structure of the new university was virtually identical with that of University College, Ibadan; the free and uninhibited drafters of the constitution of Nigeria's first independent university copied the very words devised by the colonial power in London.

But the constitution did not stay this way. Three years later the American fairy godmother now known as A.I.D. (Agency for International Development) expressed an interest in the project and entrusted to Michigan State University the responsibilities of an academic midwife. But the Eastern Region still did not want to abandon the British influence, and it was arranged that a combined American-British working party should give advice on the establishment of the university, and if possible embody in its curriculum and examinations some cooperative scheme sponsored by two universities: Michigan State and London, a mixture not conducive to homogeneity. The labours of this working party were followed by a White Paper issued by the Eastern Region government in 1958, announcing that a site had been chosen, an architect appointed, and funds secured from the Eastern Region Marketing Board to cover initial capital expenditure.[74]

In April 1959, the Provisional Council described in the 1955 act was appointed; but even before then the plans of the Eastern Region government for the new university were well advanced. At that stage it became the Provisional Council's responsibility, and not the Eastern Region government's, to take charge of the planning. This circumstance doubtless precipitated the amendment to the University of Nigeria Law, 1955, which appeared forthwith. Two months after the appointment of the Provisional Council, on 4 June 1959, a "Law to Amend the University of Nigeria Law" was enacted. It is a very brief document about a few technical points, such as auditing, power to co-opt, and investments; and tucked away in it is this sentence, referring to the University Provisional Council which—in the act of 1955—was to be "the supreme governing body" of the university: "The Minister [of Education] may give directions of a general or specific character as to the exercise and performance of [the Council's] functions, and the Council shall give effect to such directions."[75] In brief, sovereignty was transferred from an autonomous Provisional Council to the Minister of Education. But this was not the end of the story. On 14 December 1961, the final approval was given to "A Law to Consolidate the Laws Relating to the University of Nigeria."[76] The title of the law is singularly inappropriate; far from consolidating the pattern of constitution set out in 1955, it substitutes a totally different one: a constitution modified (according to the preamble) in the light of "experience gained in operating the university since its inception." This document is important; to compare its structure with that of the act of 1955 is to observe the very process of university government adapting itself to African conditions; and the process is all the more significant because it is known that the adaptation was performed under the personal supervision of one of Africa's great leaders and intellectuals, Dr. Azikiwe.

What, then, is disclosed by the so-called consolidating act of 1961? The objects and powers of the university remain unchanged, and are indeed identical with those drawn up for University College, Ibadan. It is the points of concentration of power which are changed. The University Council regains sovereignty over the university: it is no longer subject to directives from the Minister of Education. In view of the composition of the Council this is not surprising; for the Council is presided over not by a mere chairman but by

an executive chancellor appointed for life, who is none other
than Dr. Azikiwe, now President of the Republic. The
membership of the Council has shrunk from nineteen to
nine; two of the nine are the chancellor and the vice-chancellor; of the seven members who are not ex-officio, five are
appointed by the Eastern Region government and the other
two represent the academic Senate. Even assuming that the
vice-chancellor has freedom of action, there is always an
overwhelming government majority. Much of the day-to-
day business is delegated to a Finance and General Purposes
Committee. In the 1955 act not less than two members of
this committee were to be academics; in the 1961 act academics are excluded altogether: all the appointed members
must be from among the government nominees on Council.
In the 1955 act provision was made for the customary distribution of power between lay Council and academic
Senate: the function of the Senate was to "manage the
educational affairs of the University and to act for the University in all academic matters." In the 1961 act these functions are withdrawn: the Senate is now simply "responsible
to the Council" for the supervision of academic matters,
and one of its vitally important powers under the 1955 act—
to recommend the names of persons to fill vacancies on the
academic staff—is withdrawn. Its membership is less democratic too: the 1955 act provided for two nonprofessorial
members elected by all the staff (Congregation) and for
other co-opted members; the 1961 act withdraws these provisions, and the Senate is now reduced virtually to a committee of professors. The faculty boards have their wings
clipped: their functions are all subject "to the directions of
the Vice-Chancellor"; so is their composition; and (as the

straw blew in the wind in the 1955 act) they are not even permitted to elect their deans: the lay Council does that for them.

The reasons for these changes are set out clearly in a memorandum attached to the draft bill prepared for the 1961 act. It says, "Whilst the principles of academic freedom are highly cherished and shall be scrupulously maintained and respected at the University, it is essential that the powers of its policy-making sector should be clearly defined." The powers are indeed clearly defined: not only clearly defined but concentrated in the lay Council, and deliberately so, for the memorandum goes on to explain how the excessive concentration of power in the Senates of British universities is not appropriate for Nigeria. Academics should not be burdened with executive and administrative responsibilities; they should devote their full time to teaching and research. Power should reside with a body "the majority of whose members are appointed by the State," for the State represents the electorate and the electorate pays for the university.

The arguments which failed to modify the constitution of the University of Ibadan succeeded in modifying the constitution of the University of Nigeria. They are arguments which are repugnant to British professors, who are apt too readily to assume that this pattern of government is incompatible with academic freedom. In point of fact, the University of Nigeria Act, 1961, does not expose the university to interference from the State any more than the universities in Germany or France or Belgium are exposed; and academic freedom is not dead in these countries. As in England, so in Nigeria, the freedom of the universities depends on the conventions which accompany the statutes much more than on the statutes themselves. One hopes that in the University of Nigeria these conventions will be worked out. The conventions have made a shaky start. Contrary to the wishes of the Senate, the Council has rejected the proposal to have external examiners to safeguard standards; and recently it was the Council, without consulting the faculty boards, which decided on the quotas of students which should be admitted to each faculty. However, there are hopeful signs of good conventions too. When the time came in 1962 for the election of deans of faculties, for instance, the Council did indeed appoint the deans as the statutes of the university require; but the Council had before it names recommended by meetings of the faculty boards, and these recommendations were accepted.

Nigeria, then, is experimenting with two kinds of university constitution: a novel one at Nsukka and conventional British ones in the other four universities. But the essential point, the point of overriding importance to my theme, is that at no stage—apart from temporary and minor aberrations—has Nigeria repudiated the tradition of university autonomy inherited from Britain. There have been petulant complaints from Africans that the universities ought to be brought directly under State control, but governments in Nigeria have not yielded to those complaints. All one can discern are signs that the equilibrium of power will be shifted from the academics to the lay governing body, but the lay governing body still remains formally independent of the State. The African State, as it is manifested in Nigeria, seems anxious to adopt conventions similar to those which ensure the freedom of universities in Britain. Thus responsi-

bility for distributing federal grants to the Nigerian universities has been entrusted to an independent commission, similar
in concept and structure to the University Grants Committee in Britain. This commission is meticulously careful to
respect the autonomy of the universities; its conduct toward
them is above reproach; it has already acquired, among
academics, respect and a considerable influence and prestige.

Ghana. By contrast, the Ghanaian variant of the African
State has not accepted the heritage of conventions which
exempt British universities from State control. The impact
of nationalism on the university in Ghana has already been
described by witnesses who have experienced its operation.
With great sympathy and understanding, Adam Curle has
traced the melancholy story,[77] which first became notorious
in 1959, a couple of years after independence. At that time
Dr. Nkrumah's office issued directives to the University
College requiring changes in the system of leave-passages to
Britain, and in other matters internal to the college. The
college staff, "constantly on the alert for infringements of
academic freedom," resisted these directives. The attacks
from the government were not pressed home; they were
(Adam Curle says) "more like the skirmishes of a recon-
naissance party testing defensive strength, than actual as-
saults." As the college mobilised (sometimes none too
tactfully) its defences, the government came to regard it—
especially its students—as a focus of dissent and a threat to
the solidarity of the new nation. The expatriate academic
staff were said by politicians who criticised them "to do no
work which was of the slightest use to Ghana, and worst of
all to pervert the flower of her youth, filling their minds

with pernicious non-African rubbish." The ideals of high standards, quality and disengagement from political affairs, for which David Balme had worked so effectively, were dismissed as the machinations of neocolonialism. The first real assault on the autonomy of the college occurred in May 1961, shortly before the college achieved the status of an independent university. The circumstances are best described in the words of an eyewitness:

> Then late in May an undated letter (actually dispatched on the 22nd of the month) was received by the Principal from the President's Office. The main burden of this communication was that in the circumstances of transmuting the University College into a University "all appointments of members of the academic staff will automatically be terminated." Those who wished to apply for re-appointment must do so by June 10th. A further letter dated May 27th indicated that persons would be re-appointed without re-applying, but that it might "be necessary to terminate certain appointments and to revise the conditions of service of others."
>
> These letters and the exchanges, both official and unofficial, to which they led, indicated that the President had at last decided to intervene in the affairs of the College, to get rid of persons who were for one reason or another undesirable, and to arrange for closer Government (or party) control of the institution.[78]

This clumsy intervention provoked a storm of protest, not only within the college but from all over the world. "The incident . . . illustrates [said *The Times* a few days later] with discomforting clarity the vagaries of the wind to which Ghanaian politics are exposed. It appears that the original proposal, which was put to President Nkrumah by Mr. Geoffrey Bing, the Attorney General, was acted upon before anyone had had a chance to consider it."[79] The

Ghanaian leaders realised they had blundered, and over the next few weeks they tried to smooth the matter over and to offer reasonable contracts to the great majority of the academic and administrative staff. But, in the event, six appointments were terminated. "What mattered," as Adam Curle wrote, "was not the number: it was the fact that the Government had established a precedent for ending academic employment on non-academic grounds."

In preparation for its full and independent university status, the University College of Ghana had for a long time been preparing a constitution. Indeed the astonishingly archaic—but in some ways astonishingly successful—draft constitution which David Balme had devised as long ago as 1953 had anticipated full university status by underlining every word and phrase which would have to be changed if the college were elevated into a university. This constitution was never adopted by the government, although in the form of bye-laws the college used it as a working machinery from 1954 until 1961, so effectively that the original ordinance of 1948 was smothered under it. In 1957, Balme's successor as principal was asked to consider the constitution of the college. He proposed a pattern of government which was as much a facsimile of an English civic university as Balme's pattern was a facsimile of Cambridge. It restored sovereignty to a predominantly lay Council; over academic affairs it restored power to the professors; it diminished the influence of nonprofessorial members of staff. It substituted a hierarchy for a democracy. The draft was amended after two long sessions of discussion with the academic staff, to produce a document which incorporated some of the better features of the bye-laws under which the college had operated for five years. It was this draft which was sent to the Ghanaian government for approval, and which was summarily rejected by Dr. Nkrumah, who (it is said) himself scribbled "totally unacceptable" on his copy of the draft.

Meanwhile Dr. Nkrumah had received advice on the relations between universities and the State from another source: an international commission appointed in 1960 by the government of Ghana to advise on the future development of university education.[80] The commission's chairman was Kojo Botsio, Minister of Agriculture, and the membership included three academics from England, two from America, one Russian, and one African from Sierra Leone. The commission's proposals about relations between the State and the university rested on two main principles: that Ghanaian universities "should be able to respond to the immediate and future needs of the community" and "that they should have the greatest possible autonomy in their organisation, teaching and research." To this end the commission proposed that the governing body should be a University Council consisting of approximately one third of government nominees, one third of persons selected by the Senate from among the academic staff, and one third of persons nominated by various educational bodies in Ghana. Academic affairs should be delegated to a Senate comprising all heads of departments and in addition two nonprofessorial representatives from each department, with the further proviso that it would be desirable for each department to have at least one Ghanaian representative on the Senate. The commission proposed also (with one dissentient) that there should be a National Council for Higher Education and

Research which would plan, coordinate and finance higher education and research throughout Ghana.

These proposals amount to a modified version of the two-tier structure of government in a British civic university, and a modified version of a University Grants Committee to administer State grants. Nevertheless they did involve considerable adaptations to African conditions, although it may well be that these were adaptations conceived by a group of expatriates, for only one member of the commission was a Ghanaian.

The commission's report received a qualified approval from the Ghanaian government;[81] and on 1 July 1961 a University of Ghana Bill received its first and second readings in the parliament in Accra. The constitution in this bill represents, with the background I have described, the response of African nationalism in Ghana to the British heritage of university government. It displays unrestrained capitulation to African conditions. Let us take a glance at this document.[82] First, among the aims of the university:

In determining the subjects to be taught, emphasis should be placed upon those which are of special relevance to the needs and aspirations of Ghanaians, including the furtherance of African unity.

Then, as to its government:

The principal officers of the University shall be the Chancellor, the Chairman of the University Council, and the Vice-Chancellor . . . The President [of the Republic] shall hold the office of Chancellor and as such shall be the Head of the University . . . The Chairman of the University Council shall be appointed by the Chancellor . . . A person shall not be appointed as Vice-Chancellor unless his appointment has been approved by the Chancellor ... The governing body of the University ... shall consist of the following fifteen members:

(a) the principal officers of the University [the three specified above]

(b) four persons appointed by the Chancellor

(c) the secretary for the time being of the National Council for Higher Education and Research [by definition a Ghanaian civil servant]

(d) a person elected by a body appearing to the Chancellor to be representative of heads of secondary schools.

This accounts for nine of the fifteen members of the Council, and these nine assure the chancellor that a majority of the members is very unlikely to indulge in sustained opinions inconsistent with his own wishes. As for the rest of the Council, its composition is interesting and enlightened, namely a member elected from an African university outside Ghana, a member elected from a university outside Africa, and four academic members (a generous proportion compared with that in British civic universities) elected by the members of staff.

The Academic Board (the body which elsewhere is called the Senate) is clearly only an advisory body to the Council (according to the act it advises the Council even on the admission of students) but it does seem (according to the statutes which have since been made under the act) to have had delegated to it responsibility for the academic affairs of the university. It is a very large body with a quorum of twenty-four, and most of its business will of necessity be done by its executive and finance committees.

What features of this constitution can be regarded as incipient adaptations to African conditions? Certainly the concentration of power in the hands of one man—and that man the head of state—and his nominees, is one adaptation. It denotes the importance which African countries attach to their universities. A second interesting point is that the constitution, having secured for the government ultimate control over policy, does leave the management of the university to the academics. Thirdly, the constitution contains no threat to standards—although the party programme on education, which appeared in the press in May 1962, does have ominous phrases about abolishing an entrance examination to the university and lowering the entry standard from Higher Certificate to School Certificate; and recently it has been decreed that a pass in English is no longer necessary for a School Certificate. Fourthly, the commission's suggestion that some places on the Academic Board should be guaranteed to Ghanaians has not been incorporated in the constitution.

All in all, there seems to be room within the framework of the constitution of the University of Ghana for conventions to be established which would be satisfactory even to the most fastidious of academics. But at present it seems unlikely that these conventions will be established. For a time, quiet, sane, reasonable decisions of university policy are made. Confidence begins to be restored. The friends of the University of Ghana throughout the world begin to feel reassured. But one cannot help overhearing the strident voice of the president: "If reforms do not come from within, we intend to impose them from outside, and no resort to the cry of academic freedom . . . is going to restrain us from seeing that our University is a healthy University devoted to Ghanaian interests."[83]

Every now and again this bluster blows up into action. Thus in February 1964 the government-controlled press demanded that the universities of Ghana must be brought to heel. The universities (said the *Ghanaian Times*) "have become the fountain heads of reaction and fertile grounds for imperialist and neocolonialist subversion and counter-revolution."[84] Synthetic demonstrators, brought onto the campus in buses, paraded through the University of Ghana. Six members of the faculty were deported for "indulging in subversive activities."

Of course no university constitution is proof against this. The only comfort is that the University of Ghana will outlive the present generation of politicians.

IV. A Summing Up

In 1956 a group of African intellectuals in Leopoldville published in the journal *Conscience Africaine* a manifesto on self-government for the Congo.[85] One poignant phrase from this manifesto stands in my memory: "We wish to be civilised Congolese, not black-skinned Europeans." These words sum up the problems of universities in Africa, and the chief of these problems is not political, nor administrative, nor even educational: it is a problem in social psychology. Can Africans select what they want from European civilisation and reject the rest? Or does European civilisation in Africa behave like a dominant character in heredity, concealing the recessive indigenous African civilisation?

I think there is little doubt about the answer. European civilisation *is* dominant. Under its influence traditional African ways of life are at first concealed, and may ultimately be destroyed. But in the very process of exerting its dominance as it flows into the cities and villages of Africa, European civilisation itself becomes changed; so do the instruments of European civilisation. Many features of the change are consistent, apparently purposeful: a genuine social adaptation. The first signs of this adaptation are evident in three characteristic European institutions in Africa: parliament, church, and university. In African parliaments we see the appearance of one-party democracy. Those who are inclined to condemn this should remember that some African societies had successful one-party democratic forms of government long before Europeans took control; moreover the British did not encourage opposition parties in colonial legislatures. In African Christianity we see the appearance of bizarre sects. Some churchmen deplore these; they should remember that there were African ideas of God centuries before the missionaries came; it is to be expected that some African Christians should look to a black Christ, in the image of "our dark flesh of the black people" to be worshipped with dancing and drumming. The Church was divided long before it came to Africa. In African universities, what do we see? Only the very beginnings of the pressures which will cause adaptation; and I have tried—perhaps prematurely—to analyse some of the early effects of these pressures. It has been a superficial analysis, for it has dealt with superficial criteria: examination standards, curricula, constitutions. Here, at the visible surface of the university, we can draw certain simple conclusions.

The first conclusion is that Africans—and this is true along the whole West coast from Dakar to Leopoldville—have eagerly adopted the European university and are grateful that the models exported to them are the best the metropolitan countries could offer. There is no sign whatever that Africans, in some gesture to repudiate influences from Europe, will destroy the patterns of higher education which have been established in their countries. They acknowledge that universities are supranational. This concept of the catholicity of universities has taken root in Africa. The most vivid proofs of its dominance are to be found in Cairo and Fez; for in both these places the ancient seats of Moslem higher learning, almost twice as old as Oxford and Paris, have recently undergone a mutation and assumed the pattern of Western universities. Al Azhar in Cairo, after a millenium of Koranic studies, now has schools of business and public administration and engineering. Karawain, in Fez, which celebrated its eleventh centenary in 1960, now has a *cité universitaire*. Its buildings, its curriculum, and its teaching are coming to resemble those in a French university.

Although it has taken root in Africa, the university continues to disseminate the traditions, beliefs, and practices of Western civilization. This, of course, is its purpose, but some people, even some Africans, believe that there are no other traditions, beliefs, and practices worth disseminating, and they continue to defend the European cultural tradition against any but the most trivial adaptation to African societies.

The patterns of adaptation are already emerging. There is—as I said at the beginning—a strong element of rejection in African nationalism as it is manifested in Ghana and Nigeria. But it is a selective rejection. In their international relations Africans reject the alignments of Western politics; they show no sign of rejecting Western economics and technology. In their universities they reject all forms of Western control (there is tacit regret even over the need to accept foreign aid); they show no sign of rejecting the English language, or Western academic standards, or Western expatriate teachers. In curriculum Africans began by accepting British patterns and content, because it was necessary to do this in order to establish their universities on the gold standard of learning. But once this was assured, they grew increasingly concerned that curricula should be relevant to national needs. This concern shows itself in two ways: pressures to emphasize the utilitarian functions of the university, and pressures to incorporate into the under-graduate courses elements of indigenous African civilization: its languages and history, social and political systems, music and mythology. The two original university colleges in British West Africa were for a time unresponsive to these pressures. This unresponsiveness reacted in turn on the relations between colleges and governments. In Nigeria it undoubtedly played some part in the decision to set up the highly vocational university in the Eastern Region; in Ghana it precipitated some of the clumsy government intervention from which the universities in Accra and Kumasi still suffer.

With respect to the constitutions of universities and the relations between universities and the State, Africans are still feeling their way. Every foreign adviser, every visiting working party, every international commission tells them that universities must be autonomous and free from government control. Until recently this advice was accepted without question. But African leaders have now come to realise that autonomy is not always exercised wisely, and in a new country, although a university must not become a pawn for politicians, academic policy must be responsive to legitimate demands from the State. Africans are now seeking a formula which will allow to universities the essential academic freedoms—freedom to appoint staff, to select students, to determine standards, and to design curricula—and which at the same time will ensure that universities serve the essential needs of the State. In desiring a new formula, I am sure the African leaders are right. For the social purpose of a university in Africa differs from its traditional social purpose in Europe. In Europe universities have stood for continuity and conservation; in Africa universities are powerful instruments for change. They must, therefore, go into partnership with the State, and for this purpose they require a fresh constitutional pattern. Time alone will show whether the constitutions being tried out at present turn out to be adaptations favourable to the survival of university autonomy in African societies. As experiments in university government they lack imagination and they are ill-contrived. It would have been better (I think) if a much more fundamental experiment in relations between the university and the State relations had been devised: one which redefined academic freedom under African conditions (this has never been done in a scholarly way); which drew up a covenant between the university and the State, specifying on the one hand the powers to be delegated to the university and on the other hand the spheres of interest within the university where the State wishes to exert an influence—a covenant which deliberately *involved* politicians in the university instead of keeping them at arm's length, a covenant which set up machinery for continuous consultation between the State and the university. I believe that until something as imaginative as this is considered, Africans will suspend judgment on the traditional British university constitution, and regard with suspicion those who assert that it is a *sine qua non* for higher education. This point of view has been vividly put by Dr. Eni Njoku, vice-chancellor of the University of Lagos and one of the most distinguished intellectual leaders in Africa:

The modern university scholar is an entirely new type of person in Nigeria, not identified with any traditional role. The condition for such a type to flourish, such as academic freedom, is therefore an entirely new conception. Nevertheless, the principle of academic freedom has been accepted in Nigeria, not by itself, but as part of a university organization. Nigerians demanded a university as good as those existing anywhere else in the world. If academic freedom is a necessary element in such universities, then it must exist in the Nigerian institution too . . . Although the principle of academic freedom is accepted, it is important to realise that it has still to justify itself in the Nigerian context. It is not easy to argue that academic freedom is necessary in order to train the professional manpower required by the Nigerian society. On the contrary . . . this is the very reason why an insufficiently perceptive university should be given directions by the Government . . . The really cogent arguments for academic freedom . . . although applicable to Nigeria, are derived from other situations. The scholar has not yet fully arrived in Nigeria, and the advantages to be gained by giving him freedom are not yet obvious . . . At present it is merely one of the embellishments attached in its country of origin to an imported product.[86]

THE AFRICAN GRADUATE

Eni Njoku writes of the African university scholar. Here lies the deep problem of social psychology which I mentioned just now: "We wish to be civilised Congolese, not black-skinned Europeans." The impact of African nationalism on universities, which has been the theme of this book, is comparatively easy to describe. Much more important, but much more difficult to describe, is the impact of the European cultural tradition on the African graduate.

One of the most perceptive books ever written on the psychological impact of Western civilisation is D. O. Mannoni's study of the Malagasies.[87] In the course of his argument Mannoni makes the point that "an education confined to providing the colonial inhabitant with new tools could be very useful if it left the personality as a whole untouched and had no direct cultural import, but a culturally-biased education can disrupt the personality far more than one would expect."

Western education in tropical Africa has been, and still is, culturally biased. Neither in the schools run by missionaries nor in the universities established in conformity with the Asquith doctrine has it been the policy to confine education to "new tools": to technology and to the expertise of Western civilisation. It would in any case have been impossible to do so. You cannot import television sets and automobiles without importing the social philosophy which goes with these things. Technology is inseparable from a money economy. It assumes a competitive society. It assumes obedience to the clock. It assumes that the individual can detach himself from the matrix of his family and village, and exercise his individuality. All these assumptions are anathema to traditional African society. So, as Mannoni said, the African who seeks education has to pass through "the painful apprenticeship to individualism." He has to sever many of the roots which secure him to the soil of Africa: the stable framework of customary behaviour in the village; the reassuring cohesion of the extended family; the comforting sense of continuity with ancestors. He has to barter these for the borrowed sentiments and customs of Europe.

It would be impertinent for a European to guess how much affection for these traditional loyalties still lies hidden in the heart of an African university graduate; whether he can still feel at ease in both worlds—the old and the new; or whether he is relieved to be free from the uncompromising conformity of tribal society. But on the surface of his behaviour some observations can be made.

First there is an embarrassment, in a society which lays stress on the veneration of the elders, that the young should be leading the old. When Hugh and Mabel Smythe made a survey of the Nigerian educated élite, they found that in 1958 fewer than a quarter of the Nigerians regarded as "eminent" were over fifty years old.[88] This causes one of the strains which a European education imposes on the present generation of educated Nigerians. It is a strain which presumably will pass. But it is only one element in the larger tension which is tugging at African society. The spread of higher education in tropical Africa has driven apart the Westernised élite and the masses. The African graduate occupies the place previously occupied by the expatriate colonial administrator; he lives in the expatriate's house; he drives a similar car; he is paid on the high salary scale previously reserved for expatriates. Within five or ten years of leaving college he may find himself propelled into the permanent secretaryship of a ministry, into a position where rivalries are fierce, where idealism struggles with self-interest, where success is very uncomfortable and very precarious. From this altitude it is virtually impossible for him to remain in close sympathy with the great mass of his fellow countrymen. Part of the price which the African graduate pays for his higher education is loneliness. One often hears that the conscious aim of many Africans in seeking education is to break out of the continuum of their traditional society and to avoid the indignity of manual labour. This is doubtless true, but it does not diminish the danger and the spiritual discomfort. There is a no-man's-land between European culture and African culture. In this no-man's-land thousands of African graduates pass their lives, not assimilated to Europe yet strangers to their own folk, insufficient in numbers to form a self-sustaining intellectual community. One of the urgent tasks for education in Africa is to cut channels of communication between the intellectuals and the people, "to avoid the sense of separation of the university graduate from his much less well-educated countrymen."[89] It is not surprising that a group of Ghanaians educated in America, commenting on the luxurious amenities in the residence halls of the University of Ghana, with their porters, stewards, cleaners, and messengers, said these amenities were "extremely harmful" to the students there. Nor is it surprising that Dr. Azikiwe, in his inaugural address as chancellor to the students at Nsukka, pleaded for a democratization of higher education, to prevent the formation of an "intellectual aristocracy of snobs." And, in his customary manner, he has turned this plea into action; for at Nsukka (and, so far as I know, nowhere else in Nigeria) there are "campus jobs" which students can get, and earn three shillings an hour; nearly £5,000 was earned this way last year. Incidentally it helps them financially. But of course it does far more than that; it is an insurance against their becoming intellectually displaced persons when they go back to their homes.

All but a few African states have achieved political freedom. To achieve economic and cultural freedom they look to their universities. Engineers and scientists, doctors, economists, and schoolteachers will equip Africa to take her place in the economy of the Western world; but this alone will not suffice to harness and control the energy of African nationalism. Something more is needed. I have said that a prominent element in African nationalism is rejection. A nation cannot be built on rejection alone; there must also be affirmation; there must be Africans who can put into words not only what African nationalism rejects, but what it affirms. African intellectual life must become self-reproducing, inventing its own techniques, establishing its own values, becoming not only a recipient, but a donor, of world knowledge. The first signs of this can already be discerned. In his book, *The Human Factor in Changing Africa*, Herskovits describes the contribution to historical research which is coming from Africa, one which uses oral tradition and archaeology to supplement the written word.[90] The prime task of African intellectuals is to make African nationalism creative. To enable scholars to fulfil this task the universities of Africa must not only preserve their present loyalty to the Western tradition: they must also discover and proclaim a loyalty to the indigenous values of African society.

References

1. E. Burke, *The Works of the Right Honourable Edmund Burke,* new edn., vol. XIII (London, 1822), p. 65.

2. B. T. McCully, *English Education and the Origins of Indian Nationalism,* Columbia University, Studies in History, Economics and Public Law, 473 (New York, 1940).

3. C. W. Eliot, "The New Education," *Atlantic Monthly,* XIII (1869), 203–220, 358–367.

4. C. Kerr, *The Uses of the University,* Godkin Lectures, 1963 (Cambridge, Mass., 1963).

5. *Higher Education: Report of the Committee . . . under the Chairmanship of Lord Robbins, 1961–63* (1962–63), Cmnd. 2154, p. 91.

6. *Higher Education: Appendix Four to the Report of the Committee . . .* (1962–63), Cmnd. 2154–iv, p. 104.

7. *Higher Education: Government Statement on the Report of the Committee . . .* (1962–63), Cmnd. 2165.

8. J. A. B. Horton, *West African Countries and Peoples, British and Native: With the Requirements Necessary for Establishing That Self Government Recommended by the Committee of the House of Commons, 1865; and a Vindication of the African Race* (London, 1868).

9. E. W. Blyden, *The Aims and Methods of a Liberal Education for Africans: Inaugural Address Delivered by Edward Wilmot Blyden, LL.D., President of Liberia College, January 5, 1881* (Cambridge, Mass., 1882).

10. J. E. C. Hayford, *Ethiopia Unbound: Studies in Race Emancipation* (London, 1911).

11. *Memorandum of the Case of the National Congress of British West Africa for a Memorial Based upon the Resolutions to be*

Presented to His Majesty the King Emperor in Council through the Right Honourable the Secretary of State for the Colonies [London, 1920].

12. G. Padmore, ed., *History of the Pan African Congress,* 2nd edn., with new material (London, 1963).

13. Phelps-Stokes Fund, *Education in Africa: A Study of West, South, and Equatorial Africa by the African Education Commission, under the Auspices of the Phelps-Stokes Fund . . . ,* report prepared by T. J. Jones, New York [1922].

14. *Education Policy in British Tropical Africa: Memorandum . . . by the Advisory Committee on Native Education in the British Tropical African Dependencies* (1924–25), Cmd. 2374, xxi, 27.

15. M. J. Herskovits, *The Human Factor in Changing Africa* (New York, 1962), p. 228.

16. *Higher Education in East Africa: Report of the Commission Appointed by the Secretary of State for the Colonies, September, 1937* (1937), Non-Parl.

17. *Report of the Commission on Higher Education in the Colonies* [Asquith Commission], 1944–45, Cmd. 6647, iv, 673; *Report of the Commission on Higher Education in West Africa* [Elliot Commission], 1944–45, Cmd. 6655, v, 593.

18. G. M. Bull, "Impressions of a Medical Tour of the Eastern and Western Regions of Nigeria," *West African Medical Journal,* N.S. IX (1960), 139–144.

19. *Higher Education in East Africa: Report of the Committee Appointed by the Secretary of State for the Colonies, September, 1937* (1937), Non-Parl., p. 10.

20. *Report of the Committee Appointed in 1932 by the Governor of the Gold Coast Colony to Inspect the Prince of Wales' College and School, Achimota* (London, 1932), p. 14.

21. D. M. Balme, "Inaugural Address to First Ordinary Convocation, 2nd December 1950," *University College of the Gold Coast Notices* (1950–51), no. 5.

22. *Daily Times* (Lagos), 3 May 1955.

23. *Ibid.,* 14 May 1955.

24. *Ibid.,* 9 Jan. 1951.

25. *Ibid.,* 21 May 1954.

26. *Ibid.,* 28 Mar. 1956.

27. *Ibid.,* 7 Jan. 1960.

28. *Ibid.,* 24 Aug. 1954.

29. *Ibid.*, 31 Mar. 1955; also *A Tract on Higher Education in Nigeria* [Action Group manifesto, 1958], mimeo.

30. *Daily Times* (Lagos), 6 July 1959; also *University of Nigeria, Prospectus, 1962–63* [Nsukka, 1962], p. 12.

31. D. M. Balme, "Reflecting on Work Done," *Universitas*, III (Dec. 1957), 4–6 [text of farewell broadcast].

32. *Daily Graphic* (Accra), 7 Mar. 1958.

33. *Ghana Today*, 6 Dec. 1961, p. 2.

34. *Uganda Herald*, 19 Jan. 1950.

35. *Ibid.*, 11 Mar. 1950.

36. *Uganda Argus*, 1 Oct. 1960.

37. *Ibid.*, 24 June 1961.

38. *Ibid.*, 9 May 1962.

39. For example, (a) the speech of Mr. Justice M'Carthy in moving the second reading of "An Ordinance to Provide for the Establishment of a University College in the Gold Coast . . ." on 21 July 1948 (*Leg. Co. Deb.*, 1948, no. 2, p. 79); and (b) the speech of Mr. Kojo Botsio moving the second reading of "The University of Ghana Bill" (*Ghana Parl. Deb.*, XXIV, 31 July 1961, col. 868).

40. *Evening News* (Accra), 25 Sept. 1961.

41. *Daily Times* (Lagos), 13 Feb. 1957.

42. *Ibid.*, 21 May 1958.

43. *A Tract on Higher Education in Nigeria* [Action Group manifesto, 1958], mimeo.

44. *Uganda Argus*, 19 and 20 July 1963.

45. Dr. Nkrumah, in a speech at the University dinner on 24 Feb. 1963, *University of Ghana Reporter*, 29 Mar. 1963, pp. 155–157.

46. *Daily Times* (Lagos), 4 July 1955.

47. *Daily Graphic* (Accra), 19 Dec. 1955.

48. U. Okeke, "Educational Reconstruction in an Independent Nigeria," unpub. Ph.D. thesis, School of Education, New York University, 1955.

49. N. J. Okongwu, "History of Education in Nigeria, 1842–1942," unpub. Ph.D. thesis, School of Education, New York University, 1946.

50. *Daily Graphic* (Accra), 30 May 1953.

51. *Ibid.*, 5 May 1955.

52. *Ibid.*, 13 Dec. 1954.

53. N. Azikiwe, inaugural address quoted in *University of Nigeria, Prospectus, 1962–63* [Nsukka, 1962], p. 7.

54. Okeke, "Educational Reconstruction."

55. *Daily Times* (Lagos), 8 Feb. 1955.

56. *Ibid.*, 17 Nov. 1955.

57. *Ibid.*, 19 Mar. 1956.

58. *Daily Graphic* (Accra), 18 Feb. 1956.

59. *Ghanaian Times*, 3 Oct. 1961.

60. Nana Nketsia, quoted in *Ghanaian Times*, 29 Jan. 1962.

61. *University of Ghana Reporter*, 26 Oct. 1962, p. 18.

62. *Ghanaian Times*, 28 Dec. 1962.

63. *Ashanti Pioneer* (Kumasi), 1 Dec. 1961.

64. *University of Ibadan, General Information for Prospective Students, 1964–65 Session* (Ibadan, 1964).

65. *University College, Ibadan, Ordinance, 1954,* no. 10, A.25.

66. *University of Ibadan Act, 1962,* no. 37. A.421.

67. *Ahmadu Bello University Law, 1962,* N.N. no. 26, A.131.

68. *University of Ife (Provisional Council) Law, 1961,* W.N. no. 6, A.15.

69. *Report of the UNESCO Advisory Commission for the Establishment of the University of Lagos* (Paris, 1961), mimeo.

70. *Daily Graphic* (Accra), 18 Aug. 1956.

71. See ref. 45, above.

72. See ref. 43, above.

73. *University of Nigeria Law, 1955,* E.R. no. 23, A.123.

74. *University of Nigeria,* E.R. Official Document no. 2 of 1958.

75. *University of Nigeria (Provisional Council) (Amendment) Law, 1959,* E.R. no. 10, A.65.

76. *University of Nigeria Law, 1961,* E.N. Law no. 21, A.153.

77. A. Curle, "Nationalism and Higher Education in Ghana," *Universities Quarterly,* XVI (1961–62), 229–242.

78. *Ibid.,* p. 238.

79. *The Times* (London), 29 May 1961.

80. See *Report of the Commission on University Education, December 1960–January 1961* (Accra, 1961).

81. *Statement by the Government on the Report of the Commission on University Education,* W.P. no. 5/61.

82. *University of Ghana Act, 1961,* Act 79.

83. K. Nkrumah, *I Speak of Freedom* (London, 1961), p. 167 [Party address on the tenth anniversary of the founding of the C.P.P.].

84. *Ghanaian Times,* 6 Feb. 1964.

85. *Conscience Africaine:* Manifeste numéro spécial, juillet-août 1956.

86. E. Njoku, "The Relationship between University and Society in Nigeria," in *The Scholar and Society,* Bulletin of the Committee on Science and Freedom, 13 (Manchester, 1959), pp. 82–86.

87. D. O. Mannoni, *Prospero and Caliban: The Psychology of Colonization* (London, 1956).

88. H. H. and M. M. Smythe, *The New Nigerian Elite* (Stanford, 1960).

89. A. Curle, *Educational Strategy for Developing Societies* (London, 1963).

90. M. J. Herskovits, *The Human Factor in Changing Africa* (New York, 1962).

Index